ECOLISM

VOLUME 1

HENRI MAALOUF

https://myecocity.co.uk
mail@myecocicty.co.uk
linkedin.com/in/henrimaalouf
https://www.facebook.com/myecolism
https://twitter.com/maalouf_al

ECOLISM

BOOK ONE

Utopian
Eco-Socio-Economic System

BOOK TWO

Utopian Eco-City

Henri Maalouf

Matador
9 Priory Business Park,
Wistow Road, Kibworth Beauchamp,
Leicestershire. LE8 0RX
Tel: 0116 279 2299
Email: books@troubador.co.uk
Web: www.troubador.co.uk/matador
Twitter: @matadorbooks

ISBN 978 1788039 154

British Library Cataloguing in Publication Data.
A catalogue record for this book is available from the British Library.

Printed on FSC accredited paper
Printed and bound in Great Britain by 4edge Limited
Typeset in 11pt Minion Pro by Troubador Publishing Ltd, Leicester, UK

Matador is an imprint of Troubador Publishing Ltd

About the Author

I have lived in many countries where I interacted with various cultures, finally settled in England in 1988 and studied a course in advanced microprocessor technology (AMT) to top up my electronics engineering. Then I had to top up my vocational education with vendors' information technology (IT) qualifications – Microsoft Certified Systems Engineer (MCSE), Citrix Certified Enterprise Administrator (CCEA) and about 15 Microsoft Certified Professional (MCP) certificates – to get a relevant education that was compatible with market requirements.

I worked as an IT solutions architect, designing and implementing the latest technologies for banks, the government and global organisations. However, it seems genetic in my family to have the ability to write about history, poetry and philosophy. I combined my skills to design an Eco-socio-economic system and the new political philosophy of Ecolism.

I was happily working in IT, earning good money and was not interested in writing books, politics or knowing what democracy or capitalism actually meant. But, when the recession of 2008 hit the UK and most countries in the world, I had an awakening call. I thought there is a better way to live, in a self-sufficient, sustainable environment, providing the essentials for survival without being influenced by global economic turmoil.

Therefore, I have written this book hoping that one day people will understand that there is a better way to live in a more secure and sustainable human economic system.

My vision is to eliminate both poverty and unemployment, create a better socio-economic system and Eco-lifestyle to preserve a greener planet, create more ethical and moral civilised humanity and save it from the inevitable accelerated self-destruction.

CONTENTS

BOOK ONE
MY UTOPIAN ECO-SOCIO-ECONOMIC SYSTEM

Contents

BOOK TWO
Utopian Eco-City

CONTENTS

BOOK ONE

MY UTOPIAN ECO-SOCIO-ECONOMIC SYSTEM

Dedication
to Book One

I dedicate this book to the billions who are unemployed, deprived, elderly and disabled. I hope people have the power to select politicians and governors who will build for them Eco-cities, a better Eco-socio-economic system and an Eco-lifestyle for a more ethically advanced civilisation.

The European Union (EU), United Kingdom (UK) and the United States of America (USA) socio-economic systems are based on so-called 'capitalism' and 'democracy'. Well, how good is capitalism if economies might collapse as a result of a little instability or if the elite few have the ability to cause a recession? How good is a democracy if there is less justice for the poor and more for the rich?

There is an alternative to making the poor rich and the rich even richer without causing miseries, uncertainties and unfairness for the most impoverished. This book aims to start a trend to reform capitalistic democracy and convert it to more of social democracy, narrowing the gap between the rich and the poor for better justice, freedom and the welfare of the weakest.

The dedication of this book uses the UK, EU and the USA as examples, but the principles are the same for any country, each with varying degrees of economic and social traditions or socio-economic systems.

My heart bleeds for those who are helpless and suffer from the greed of the rich, who build their wealth on the misfortunes of others.

We hope that our politicians, the rich and the elite few listen to the voices of wisdom and ethics. That they hear the crying souls in their dungeons, who suffer from the autocracy of our democracy and learn that there is a better way to reach prosperity and justice for all.

I hope the time of enlightenment comes and the sun rises on our empires to remove its vampires.

PART 1

How to Read This Book

Ecolism is a new philosophy based on living in an Eco-environment complying with the ethical Eco-principles for a new Eco-socio-economic system, which is based on sustainable self-sufficiency, in Eco-cities or countries.

The Eco-socio-economic system is a new social and economic system that follows Ecolism's Eco-principles. The aim is to ensure self-sufficiency and sustainability, provide a greener environment, end poverty and create peaceful, compassionate societies living in a sustainable human ecosystem.

The Eco-Magna-Carta is the same as the Eco-socio-economic system, but that is applied to smaller communities and does not oppose any national socio-economic system. In other words, following the moral values of any religion or just a set of rules for a family, community, town or Eco-city.

The Eco-principles are the guidelines for all laws and rules on the planet. The books in the Ecolism series are revolutionary guidelines for changing everything people do to be more ethical. There are some Eco-principles in this book and many more in *Ecolism 3 – Eco-Principles and Lifestyle* and other publications. The essence of the Eco-principles is responsible freedom, equality, justice, moral and ethical mentalities, caring, loving and sharing. In a nutshell, a cleaner living environment, fairer justice and better human rights for everyone on the planet.

In my Ecolism series of books, there are unfamiliar words such as Ecolism, Ecolist, Ecocracy and many other nouns hyphenated with the prefix 'Eco-'. All of them mean more ethical, environmentally friendly, fairer practices or just regulations.

Ecocracy is a new name given to the new Eco-socio-economic system as an alternative to democracy, capitalism and any other socio-economic systems.

An Ecolist is a person who follows Ecolism's principles or Ecocracy and lives as a member of the Eco-society in any country, city, town or village.

'Eco' means environmentally friendly as defined by English dictionaries. But in my concept of Ecolism it means much more. It changes everything humans do into more moral and ethical practices.

'Eco-' is a prefix used as part of a compound noun or compound adjective to describe an attribute of an actor (or a noun). Contrary to the Oxford dictionary, which starts such words with a lower-case letter, in this new concept it is capitalised to recognise it as the formal name of an ethical new religion that changes everything humans do to become more ethical, environmentally friendly, honest, caring, responsibly free and morally civilised. The concept is also about living in a more sustainable, self-sufficient ecosystem for humans in communities, towns, Eco-cities, countries and continents.

The Eco-xxx words used in the Ecolism books are similar to Eco-governance, Eco-agriculture, Eco-industries, Eco-businesses, Eco-judge, etc.

Note: The author has purposely chosen not to use the Oxford comma and has not included it before 'and' and 'or' deliberately. He considers both 'and'/'or' and a comma to be a pause in a sentence. He prefers to use one pause and not two in a sentence. He believes his readers will understand the dependant and independent clauses in the sentence from the context.

Introduction

There are many parts or chapters in each Ecolism book that people could read or skip, depending on their interests. However, it is preferable that they understand all the Ecolism books and all chapters to gain an awareness of the alternatives to the standard ways of living. The concept is designed like a puzzle with many pieces; if one is missing, the picture is not complete.

I have researched some topics in more depth than others, for two reasons. The first is my lack of speciality in each matter and the second is to make it easier to read, without too much detail or technical jargon. However, subject-matter experts could follow my guidelines and help me to create entire new ecosystems and Eco-principles by participating in forums on my website. My Ecolism books aim to build public awareness about the alternatives to our socio-economic systems that can at least protect the most vulnerable and end poverty.

Therefore, I would like my readers to take part in discussions and forums on my website (myecocity.co.uk) and volunteer their ideas or expertise to help to create ethical systems to change human mentalities to more moral ones. We might be advanced in science, but are we progressive in fairer justice systems, morality, ethics, transparency, honesty and responsible freedoms? I doubt it.

The concept of the Eco-socio-economic system is to create a social ruling and economic system called Ecolism, which is better than capitalism, democracy, socialism, communism, religious doctrines and all other socio-economic systems.

Ecolism is the political philosophy of the Eco-socio-economic system, which acts as guiding principles for ethical and fairer regulatory conduct. Ecolism is a new word that can be added to the dictionary and is alternatively called Ecocracy, which is a new, reformed social democracy that is more ethical and Eco-friendlier.

The Eco-socio-economic system is mainly described in this book *Ecolism 1* and in *Ecolism 3*. However, it is complemented in *Ecolism 2*, which describes how to build Eco-city of one million Eco-homes for people to live an economic Eco-lifestyle.

The four books outline the concept of how to live self-sufficiently in a sustainable human ecosystem unaffected by global or national economic turmoil, such as what happened during the recession of 2008.

The concept reduces the cost of living to the bare necessities, to the extent of eating from the edible garden surrounding the family's Eco-home as a worst-case scenario. In Europe, there are social-welfare systems purposed to help the poor to survive when they have no income. However, the systems vary from one country to another and have never eliminated poverty or homelessness, nor have they provided a good living standard for everyone.

Countries spend billions on weapons of mass destruction and warfare, but much less on welfare. Corruption still exists in most countries; the elite few get the most, while the rest suffers the worst. *The Ecolism books find a balance between the extremes of extravagant wealth and extreme poverty.*

The Eco-city and the Eco-socio-economic system are designed to solve such unfair-minded social-welfare issues and much more. It not only saves billions on social-care budgets but also creates a more civilised and ethical Eco-welfare system.

An end to poverty, a higher living standard, peaceful living, responsible freedom and justice and equality for all are at the heart of the Eco-socio-economic system and Ecolism philosophy. I hope that, one day, humans learn to live in perfect harmony among themselves, with no greed, selfishness, megalomania or imperialism; no wars or political and economic invasion of weaker countries to achieve world domination; and no extreme wealth for the elite few only.

PART 2

Summary of Ecolism Solutions

Henri Maalouf declares:

Pay less but get more, work more to live better.

In this abstract, I outline the main benefits of the Eco-socio-economic system for people living an Eco-lifestyle in Eco-cities. The aim of this concept is to eliminate poverty and encourage governments to invest in people for a better return on investment. Each family owning an Eco-home and a decent living standard from the cradle to the grave must become compulsory human rights.

Imagine living in an Eco-home where you can farm the small area of surrounding land and eat from it instead of starving. The Eco-home is in an organised and designed Eco-city, so you do not pay for electricity, water, transport, TV, phone, insurance, solicitor fees, internet, health and other outgoings.

Imagine if the local authority has to train you on required skills and find you a job so you can repay your mortgage and live better. Otherwise, the local authority has to pay the interest on your mortgage and give you food to survive. Only then can poverty and homelessness be eliminated.

Imagine an Eco-city surrounded by Eco-industries, businesses, agriculture, entertainment, utilities, information and communications technology (ICT) data centres and others, all designed to help you live a better life. The Eco-city is open for business 24/7 and it has plenty of jobs available to work flexible hours. Also, you can work from home, study at home, have access to the internet to explore the world, become self-employed and make your living. Imagine if the rich invest in the wellbeing of the poor, the poor become rich and the rich get reasonably richer, narrowing the gap of wealth between them.

Imagine if the justice system does not consider the interests of the rich and powerful as more important than the welfare of the poor. Imagine if the justice system acts like God, who can know the truth and everybody is equal as it would be on the judgment day. Imagine, if owning an Eco-home (for each family) is a compulsory human right.

Imagine millions of people living in an Eco-city as a big family, caring for each other and supporting the wellbeing of each one of them. Imagine if the Eco-city is run as an efficient conglomerate that has to take care of those families from the beginning till the end. Raising, educating, training and paying them equally to cover their cost of living to make the conglomerate successful.

Only then can you become a productive, civilised, free human with equal rights to others and living in a more dignified way.

The Ecolism series of books stretches your imagination on how to make it happen, as a revolutionary concept of a new Eco-socio-economic system. The Ecolism concept is perhaps an aberration or beyond the comprehension or care of some people, civil servants, politicians, ministers or lords. But, in time, as humans evolve, they will learn that there are better ways for humans to live in peace in a human ecosystem. Evolution and progress in life entail major changes in environmental circumstances, traditions and replacing the old systems with new ones.

The revolutionary solutions to the problems caused by capitalism and autocratic democracy are the answers to the public's wishes. There is a wave of rising populism asking for change, but they do not know how to make this happen. Ecolism shows them the way. I hope the day of enlightenment comes and that welfare prevails against warfare. I hope that justice becomes like the divine judgment day when all sinners and money worshippers are reformed, especially those in authority or who are rich and influential.

The concept lessens the need for the government to spend billions to support the destitute and, at the same time, it guarantees a better living standard for the impoverished. However, the balance of giving and taking must be maintained for a system to succeed and remain ethical. Hence, a fair assessment of people's abilities to work is essential for training them in the required skills and finding them suitable jobs to contribute more and live better.

In the Eco-socio-economic system, it is the government's responsibility to find jobs for the locals first. Otherwise, they must subsidise their costs of living and not just provide a percentage of it. It is like a family: all of them work and subsidise each other to sustain their dignified survival.

In a competitive world, with billions on the planet living at various standards, it becomes essential to reduce the cost of living to accept lower wages and become more competitive. Besides, working smarter, harder and longer gives people an advantage. Therefore, training to higher levels and in the required skills should accompany workers throughout their lives so they may adapt to the required jobs. The more you know, the further you go.

Investing in people pays off. Give them more so that they can contribute more. Crucially, it is ethical to ring-fence the minimum cost of living to support people with lesser abilities to survive in a dignified way and with a higher living standard. *The higher the minimum living standard a government can provide to its people, the more civilised the country becomes.* Therefore, in *Ecolism 2 – Utopian Eco-city* and *Ecolism 4 – Utopian Eco-Home,* I detail the minimum living standard required.

Building an Eco-home for each family might look difficult to some people. It might be true in small countries that have a small amount of land, rough terrain of mountains or hardly any money. But it is not difficult for a rich country that has less than 10% of its people living on its land. Agriculture no longer needs a vast area of land, because we can grow food in all seasons and vertically in greenhouses and domes. Preserving the 'green belt' or countryside scenery is not more important than accommodating people in Eco-homes.

In the United Kingdom (UK), building an Eco-home, especially in an Eco-city or Eco-town would save the government billions or 75% of their spending on housing benefits.

Currently, in the UK as an example, there are about 18 million claimants for various types of social benefits costing the ministerial Department for Work and Pensions (DWP) about £120 billion/year. In the UK, people on no or low income claim money for housing benefits in addition to social care. The DWP in the UK pays £12 billion/year for rented accommodation, in addition to another £12 billion for various types of social housing.

If the DWP wants to save 75% on housing benefits, the formula is simple. An Eco-home costs £100,000 to build and the interest on its mortgage is 1.5 to 3% maximum. The monthly mortgage interest is £125 to £250/month compared to paying about £1,000/month for rented accommodation.

This is on the basis of one million families claiming for rented accommodation about £1,000/month on average or £12,000/year. It costs the DWP £12 billion a year. In comparison, the interest on mortgaged accommodation costs £3 billion/year. Therefore, the DWP could save £9 billion/year if they pay interest on the mortgage instead of paying for rented accommodation. Similar savings can be achieved for other social-care benefits when people live in Eco-cities spend less on their outgoings and enjoy a higher living standard.

Building an Eco-city of one million Eco-homes would cost £100 billion and probably about £20 billion in addition for its infrastructure. The cost might not look easily achievable. Actually, it is easily achievable with government borrowing or quantitative easing for banks. If a government borrows £120 billion at 1% interest rate, the cost is only £12 billion and, as I mentioned previously, the DWP saves £9 billion on housing benefits. Therefore, it is the best investment for borrowing money, unlike borrowing for a high-speed train project or similar.

However, to encourage investors to lend to the unemployed living on income support, the government must guarantee the mortgage loan.

Additionally, the government must donate publicly owned land, which can be used as a deposit to lend 100% of the loan. Knowing how banks and financial institutions behave, the mortgage loans must be controlled by an Eco-bank created to look after the Ecolists welfare.

The Eco-city project needs a bold government with a great vision and ethical thinking to support people with low or no income in better ways. Moreover, adopting the right policies to stop wasting the taxpayers' money is required.

The DWP in the UK would rather spend hundreds of

millions on solicitors and bureaucracy to deal with appeal cases against the disabled for underpaying their entitlements. Also, they have recently scrapped the support for mortgage interest (SMI) and prefer to pay for rented accommodation instead of interest on a mortgage, which is three times higher. Isn't it wise or ethical to pay the disabled and pensioners their rights instead of paying it to solicitors and for bureaucratic micromanagement to get away with not paying them their rights?

Furthermore, the Eco-socio-economic system and the Eco-city, with its surrounding businesses and industries, are designed to employ the unemployed, including the retired and partially disabled. Therefore, the unemployed will have the incentive to work and repay the mortgage, to build up equity and enjoy a better retirement. As a bonus, people might become more productive, work more, earn more and pay more taxes. As a result, they can pay back the government-borrowed money to build one million Eco-homes.

Different locations have varied costs of living. Therefore, building standard Eco-cities or Eco-towns, accompanied with a standard Eco-lifestyle in an Eco-socio-economic system, will standardise the costs of living. *Once the cost of living for an Eco-lifestyle becomes standard and known, then an accurate subsidy for it becomes universal and can be fairly implemented.*

Finally, imagine if the United States of America (USA) creates peace on earth and stops spending more than $700 billion each year on weapons of mass destruction. The USA could build Eco-cities in each state and give an Eco-home to every poor family. Every American would be rich from such projects, including the political parties. Obviously, everybody else in the world should follow suit to maintain the balance of peace on earth and become more morally civilised.

When I was in Sweden, I witnessed a parade for the socialist party and, when I asked a Swedish person about political parties, he said that in Sweden everybody is socialist, but one is more than the other. In my view, this is how each country should be, racing to become more socialist than capitalist or at least reform democracy and make it fairer to the poorer.

Therefore, Henri Maalouf declares: *The more social you are, the more civilised you become.*

PART 3

Ecolism Philosophy

Henri Maalouf declares:

Religions have merged gods into one, Ecolism unites the religions into one.

Ecolism is my creation of a new, ethical socio-economic system that balances power among the poor, the rich and rulers. It is not designed for an Eco-city only but can be implemented anywhere else in the world with some variations to suit each culture.

Ecolism is the balance of the extremes between conflicting ideologies and socio-economic systems, such as communism and capitalism, in addition to extracting the best of all other ideological socio-economic systems or 'isms'.

Note: By 'isms', we mean capitalism, communism, socialism, totalitarianism, Buddhism, Judaism, Hinduism, Sikhism and atheism, but also democracy, Islam, Christianity and all the other sects of religions and the variations of the world's socio-economic systems since history began.

Ecolism is a new concept or a religion, of an Eco-socio-economic system that extracts the moral values and ethical principles from all faiths and ruling regimes. It narrows the big gap between the rich and poor, limit the powers of rulers, yet proportionately balances and distributes the wealth, power and responsible freedom among them all.

The followers of Ecolism could live in either an Eco-city or an Eco-community under the new Eco-socio-economic system, following the ethical Eco-principles described in the series of Ecolism books.

Most regimes of the socio-economic systems or 'isms' throughout the centuries are likely to have some sound principles in them. However, they also have abusers of the laws and have failed to provide optimum justice, true equality and responsible freedom for everyone to live happier lives in a sustainable and secure human ecosystem from birth till death.

Ecolism is a new Eco-socio-economic system, which is self-sufficient, self-governed, sustainable and organised to formulate a new way of living in a more-civilised human ecosystem, unaffected by political, religious or financial influences.

Ecolism does not impose its will or systems on others, neither does it accept the influences of other systems. However, with an open mind, it could logically assess what would be best for the Ecolists to evolve to an advanced form of more-civilised existence.

Ecolism means to live better and consume less, avoid unnecessary waste, reuse before recycling, give others what you do not need and help the Ecolists to live in a better Eco-socio-economic system.

Ecolism believes that every human is a valuable asset and recognises identity, regardless of status in society. It is the responsibility of the wealthiest and rulers to ensure that the necessities for survival in our demanding world are freely available for everyone as a minimum human right. In return, people must work and become productive to pay for a dignified way of life in an Eco-socio-economic system.

The Eco-socio-economic system does not deprive the poor of the necessities, such as warm accommodation, nutritious food, communication means, continuous education or training in skills, health and social care, security and protection. At least, it gives people what they reasonably need without extravagance or greed. It is unlike democracy, which is trying to do all the above but failing to do so for everyone, under the influence of capitalism and the narcissistic greed for money.

In our modern and demanding world, communication means, such as the internet, computers, phones and transport, are necessities that everybody needs to survive to a reasonable standard of living. Front-line services, such as free healthcare, education, skills training and unemployment benefits, are indispensable for sustaining the social ecosystem.

The minimum pre-requisites for modern living are a decent home, water, electricity, food and security, which are critical for the self-sufficiency and sustainability for each one of us to survive in a competitive world.

Ecolism does not treat the poor as helpless or slaves and impose on them further penalties to intensify their misery. Instead, it treats them as the children of life, learning to grow and cope with a demanding civilisation; helps them to solve their problems; and re-educates them to adapt and thrive in a harmonised society.

It is like what Jesus Christ said: "Those who never sin, let them throw the first stone." The wisdom that comes out of what Jesus said and its application to modern life in the 21st century is that everyone makes mistakes (or sins), fails or offends in an imperfect socio-economic system. That does not mean penalties are the answer, but, instead, we should reform, re-educate and remove the root causes. So, this is the best answer for a better solution to prevent the reoccurrence of social problems.

Ecolism's principles advocate selecting Eco-city councillors or leaders according to their academic qualifications, achievements, abilities, merits, specialisations, ethics and track records of achievements. Then, whichever candidate is chosen by the majority of the Ecolists, based on their manifesto or a promise to deliver what is better for the community, the Ecolists decide if they want to elect that candidate.

It is also the Ecolists' voting majority that can remove leaders from power when they abuse their trust and do not fulfil their pledges. Eco-councillors do not autocratically appoint any person in authority whose decisions affect others but propose candidates who meet the specified criteria of selection, then leaders are elected and deselected by a majority, depending on their achievements or failure.

One might say, "Well, democracy is like that, what is new!" In my opinion, democracy is becoming autocracy in the name of the law that is designed to favour the elite few and the rich. The proof is in the outcome, not in what is announced and, as always, the devil is in the details. The truth is not in what you hear; it is hidden behind what you do not know or prove. The cat might lick abrasive sandpaper that causes blood to be drawn from its tongue. It thinks, it is delicious food, but, in fact, it is the blood from its tongue, not the sandpaper.

The essence of freedom in Ecolism is the consensus on disciplinary rules and principles that treat humans with balanced equality. The rulers cannot play the role of God and solely impose policies without people's agreement or approval. Legislating a principle or policy without people's consent becomes an autocracy that appears to be a democracy.

The wealthy and powerful should be equal to the weak and helpless. The more powerful should not take advantage of people's weaknesses and deprive them of their responsible freedom and equal rights. The prime minister or president of the greatest country is equivalent to a rubbish collector when it comes to human rights, liberty and justice.

The religions say we are all equal before God and democracy claims that we are all equal facing justice. However, is this claim true for everyone? The rich and influential always manipulate the justice system and get away with their sins. The solicitors defend clients for their money, not because they are right or wrong. The judges' justification for a judgment depends on their moods, politics and the technicalities, but not the purpose of the laws in most circumstances.

Ecolism has no racism or favouritism and places the right people in the right jobs based on their merits, not on their colour, status, gender or race.

Ecolism is the new Eco-society for the future of humanity, with the right to live free but responsibly and the right to live secure, self-sufficient and cared for from birth till death. Ecolism does not believe in prison sentences or punishment but believes in removing the root causes of failure, reforming or re-educating those who fail and reintroducing them as reformed members of the Eco-society.

PART 4

Ecolism Comparison

The purpose of Ecolism is to create a new Eco-socio-economic system purposed to end poverty and provide a self-sufficient, sustainable Eco-lifestyle for Eco-communities or Eco-cities. It is mainly to protect the poorest, the elderly and the most vulnerable on the planet by providing them with a decent living standard as a minimum requirement for their human right to live in an Eco-home in a self-sufficient ecosystem.

Ecolism principles apply to its followers, but it is best if implemented in a sizeable utopian Eco-city designed for an Eco-society that accepts living an Eco-lifestyle. The ultimate objective of Ecolism is to reform democracy and other socio-economic systems or at least to give the poorest a better chance to live in peace, happiness, harmony, security, economic stability and with a better social-welfare system.

To better understand the Ecolism philosophy, it is best to compare it with other socio-economic systems. All the socio-economic systems are not perfect and may not become perfect. The proof is in the poverty, wars, limitation of freedoms and injustices that existed for thousands of years and still exist in the 21st century. Whenever there is conflict, there is an injustice for one or the other. Therefore, a balanced system resolves such strife. Thus, our humanity needs a new Eco-socio-economic system that balances the extremes and removes the root causes of conflicts.

So, let us compare Ecolism with other socio-economic systems.

Capitalism versus Ecolism

Capitalism in the 21st century and earlier is controlled by the rich or the so-called capitalists. It has become an authoritarian socio-economic system that controls national policies and principles, disregarding the ethics of democracy and comprehensive social welfare. The practices of capitalism are profits at any cost, regardless of consequences or fairness to others.

The philosophy of capitalism is the private ownership of commodities and assets, treating human resources as robotic working machines that produce profits. The dominance of capitalism and global organisations in the West became hugely influential, able to manipulate or control political systems and capable of trembling the economies of the most powerful nations.

Capitalism allows the rich to manipulate politicians with financial contributions to their parties or by lobbying them to legislate for national projects that suit their vested interests at the expense of taxpayers' money. Sometimes, it is secret bribery for decreeing what suits the interests of the rich, even if it causes more misery to the poor.

The politicians manipulate the electorates with false promises, like false prophets and misleading information to justify the feasibilities of such national projects that are supposed to be better for the public, more cost-effective and better value for the taxpayers' money.

Most people either do not care, can't be bothered, do not know the truth or are just believers of the false prophets taking the form of a prime minister, president, party leader or member of parliament (MP). There are those who know, care and petition, but they are a drop in the ocean of the political and financial power and have no impact.

Capitalists mainly support two political parties and it does not matter which party people elect because they can influence both. It is common in the USA, UK, Germany, France and many other countries where capitalists are the real power behind the scenes.

However, there are many similarities between the monopoly of governance and the manipulation of the nation that yield the same results. The Chinese ruling system is one communist party, the Russian system is totalitarianism, others are dictatorial and some are monarchical. While democracies' two parties are controlled by capitalists and the results are the same in all of them.

When we go to a supermarket to shop freely for the available products, we are still under the influence of that supermarket's products. And if all supermarkets buy from the same source and fix the prices between them, then it becomes an illusion that we are free to choose what we want and get good-value-for-money products. The analogy means that if the source or the controlling power is capitalism, then it does not matter which leader the people choose.

Capitalism forcibly snatches more from the poor to satisfy the narcissistic greed of the rich, manipulating and abusing the principles of democracy, which have become the rules of autocracy. It forever widens the gap between rich and poor and takes true freedom and justice away from the poor.

If this trend continues, there will be only a handful of people with enormous wealth and the rest are below the poverty lines. The longer this trend continues, the more pressure will be on people to explode and destroy it all because they will have nothing more to give and nothing else to lose.

Ecolism, in comparison, democratises and socialises capitalism by equalising powers among people, governors and capitalists. Distributing the powers is logical, in the long term, to keep the status quo of the Eco-socio-economic system and sustain the coexistence of mutual benefits for all.

Each authority requires the other two to maintain its existence. In other words, the workforce needs investors to establish a business or industry and the governors' role is to regulate them both. But the public elects the governors and votes them out upon failure or misconduct and the governors can do the same to failing businesses or their executives, while the investors can decide whether to remain or leave without causing harm to the workforce and the continuity of the human ecosystem.

In the Ecolism political system, the electorate can deselect or remove politicians from power and the workforce can remove their chief executive officers (CEOs) from their position upon failure or misconduct, with no compensation or bonuses. The politicians or government controls and enforces disciplinary actions on businesses and people for any offence or misconduct. The workforce cannot strike and cause a loss of profits for businesses or earn money without working and being productive.

Businesses and investors have the government's protection for their investment and an agreed minimum margin of tax-free profits but pay taxes on earnings above the allowed tax-free threshold, in addition to paying an agreed minimum hourly rate for the required skills or training local employees in the needed jobs.

If the trends of inequality, injustice and increased poverty continue, they will reach the point of no return. The time may come for the volcano to erupt and burn its green surroundings, unless we create newer and fairer social ecosystems that are just for everyone on the planet.

It is already happening in countries where there is extreme totalitarianism and there is even a split in Western societies into two opposing parties: one supporting the rich to get richer and supporting their vested interests and the other opposing party that gives more to the poor but is not doing enough. People have started to elect whoever is against the status quo of the establishment or the envisaged new world order.

It is as we saw in the Brexit vote in the UK, in electing President Trump in the USA and whatever will happen next in the rise of populism and the future of the European Union (EU).

Democracy versus Ecolism

What is the definition of democracy? The dictionary defines it as a form of government in which the supreme power is vested in the people and exercised directly by them or by their elected agents under a free electoral system.

We always hear politicians talking about democracy, freedom, equality, etc. However, although it means people are free to elect any candidate they choose, they do not have the liberty to deselect that candidate when he or she betrays their trust. Politicians talk about legislating for voting out or removing an MP from power if the electorate chooses to do so, but they never actually do it, unless there is a media scandal of some sort.

There is no principle to remove a prime minister or president from power, even if he or she destroys the country's economy or signs a treaty surrendering the sovereignty and principles of the country to another. In my view, that is not a democracy and it does not exist in practice, only on paper.

The free electoral system allows the electorate to choose any candidate they like. Fair enough. However, there are only two main parties and most people take sides with one or the other, even if both are corrupted or influenced by global organisations, secretive clubs, more powerful countries or party donors.

The media always split people's opinion between the two parties without an alternative third or fourth party. It gets worse when both parties and the media work against any upcoming third party that causes a threat to either of the dominant two.

The problem with parties is the limited choice and, whichever MP the people choose, he or she must follow the party line or the leader.

Of course, there are the occasional rebels in each party who do not follow orders from the party whip, but they cannot influence the leader in one direction or another because they are a minority, unless they hold the balance of power.

Democracy is no longer a social system of equality allowing people to have a say in political decisions and what affects their lives. Although people can vote and select their leaders, whoever assumes the dominant power automatically becomes influenced by business conglomerates and implements policies to suit their vested interests, disregarding the consumer or the public will.

Some politicians become influenced by more powerful countries, executing their treaties, interests and global agendas without consulting people on critical issues and most people do not know any better anyway. Even if a leader grants people the right to vote in a referendum, the leader tries to influence the results.

However, in some democratic countries, such as the UK,

the USA and other EU countries, to protect the nation against tyranny or the dominance of one political power, the legislation creates the separation of powers into three divisions a '*trias politica*' or 'tripartite governance'.

Typically, the three governance divisions are the legislature, executive and judiciary. No one division can have total control. The government in the UK consists of the executive branch (the prime minister and ministers), the legislative branch (the House of Commons and the House of Lords) and the judiciary (the courts).

However, a prime minister sometimes has the authority to exercise prerogative powers without consulting Parliament. It is the party leader with the majority who can practically do anything unless substantial numbers of MPs drop their support.

The USA has a similar system and the constitution splits the powers among the legislative, executive and judicial branches.

But the president also appoints judges and officials to support him/her, in addition to having the backing of the majority of his/her party in Congress and has some executive powers to veto a bill or law enhancement.

There is a comparable situation in the EU, where the EU Council, the EU Commission and the EU Parliament are linked in a similar form of governance. However, the president of the EU is not publicly elected and the rest of the commissioners have to take an oath to serve the EU and not the interests of their countries! So, there is no democracy in the EU. Hopefully, one day it will change and there will be more democracy in the EU.

Similarly, in most countries, there are three governance branches and some are better than others. However, there are always lobbyists behind the scenes influencing the ones in power. The point is, the manipulation and abuse of powers still exist, regardless of the checks and balances of the various governance powers. The proofs of this are the injustices, inequalities, freedom limitations and the existence of poverty in a high percentage of the public.

While Ecolism, in comparison, allows people to elect leaders who pass the criteria for selection, which defines an ethical track record, qualifications, expertise and abilities. But it also allows them to remove the elected leaders from power upon any misconduct, failure to serve the national and public interests or utterly failing to deliver the promised manifesto.

The citizens have the right to be consulted on any policy or changes to the socio-economic system that affect their lives. It is like a codified constitution that cannot be changed without a referendum and cannot be overridden by presidential executive orders.

However, the traditional voting system on paper is expensive and not suitable for use in voting on regular changes in policies. Therefore, using an electronic voting system is more cost-effective and can be designed as a tamper-proof system. The public survey polls guide politicians to go in the right direction.

In Ecolism, petitioning to remove politicians, company CEOs or anyone in authority is non-debatable. Once it reaches the majority percentage threshold, it takes immediate effect. Upon any proof of misconduct, no one is immune from prosecution and trial.

In the current socio-economic system, there are many people in power who have extra privileges, are unaccountable and can afford lengthy trials to avoid prosecution.

In Ecolism, every activity is recorded and open to the public. It is real transparency and everyone, without exception, is accountable and subject to prosecution.

Socialism versus Ecolism

Socialism means distributing power and wealth among the proletariat (workforce, rulers and capitalists), but it fails to determine where to draw the line between them or create a balanced formula that is accepted and implemented by them all.

However, a version of it is still in use by Scandinavian countries and in most of Europe under different names, such as social welfare or benefits systems applied in one form or another, but we are not sure for how long.

Many front-line services were nationalised and have gradually become privatised. In time, capitalism might privatise national health, education and whatever will be left from social benefits and front-line services for the poor.

Some of Karl Marx's theories were feasible and great, but were abused by the Russian leaders Lenin and Stalin by converting socialism to communism and the totalitarianism of the ruling communist party. However, the social benefits of the welfare system, which is still adopted today in some European countries, are the results of Karl Marx's work.

Ecolism goes a step further and asserts that a decent living standard is a compulsory human right for the incapable, unemployed and retired.

Ecolism must give the investor an incentive to invest to guarantee jobs for the workforce (the proletariat) and give the worker the incentive to work harder and smarter to earn more and live better. It disciplines the investor and employee to follow beneficial mutual rules to maintain the status quo, where the rich or investor gets a reasonable return on investment, while the worker gets a fair return on productivity. As a result, the investor's profits and the workforce's productivity generate taxes to be spent on the welfare of society to guarantee the sustainability of the human ecosystem.

Communism versus Ecolism

Communism, with all its variations in Russia, China, Cuba and the totalitarianism of North Korea, has created classless societies living on the basic necessities for survival. The socio-economic system provides free, rationed food, basic accommodation, simple clothes and a good education, but forces the individual to work in factories or do specific administrative jobs.

Such a socio-economic system has made people the property of the government and is controlled by a single ruling communist party. The public act as robots programmed by the government to perform specific tasks dictated by the republic. A robot is an executor and has no incentive or motivation to do anything beyond its program.

Nevertheless, the system has created powerful countries with industrial and nuclear power that costs much less than what it costs the USA to produce. The communist regime had ensured that the basic necessities to survive are provided to everyone and there was no homelessness, starvation or poverty, as there is in Africa. On the other hand, there has been no further progressive improvement of productivity to compete with the freer Western capitalistic systems.

As always in history, the ideology was abused by the rulers and created an enormous gap in wealth and power between the working class and the ruling communist party. Eventually, the communist systems were isolated economically and socially from the free world of capitalism. The isolation led to the political and economic collapse of the Soviet Union and forced the rulers to adopt a more flexible and open socio-economic system.

A similar economic failure happened in China until the ruling communist party decided to be more open to the world, reduce bureaucracy and tight controls and then compete with the West to improve its economy. This is in contrast with North Korea, where the strict public control still exists and so there are lower standards of living, global isolation, limited resources and poverty.

The conclusion from the above is that when rulers impose more controls, increase bureaucracy and limit the freedom of the population, then the economy and progress became limited. The economy collapses and the entire system fails. It is like an overdraft facility from a bank in that if it is limited, then the borrower will have a smaller trading capability, but if the credit facility is more significant, then the trading capability increases.

While communism is too limiting but is fairer in providing the minimum standard of living, capitalism is not limiting but does not guarantee a minimum standard of living or end poverty and homelessness. Therefore, Ecolism balances the two extremes, ensures a better standard of living as a minimum, encourages ambitions to the maximum and restricts inequalities.

Religions versus Ecolism

Some religious systems have failed to adapt to the current 21st century's socio-economic systems and integrate with the liberties of modern social convictions. And, as there is a big gap between the super-rich and the super-poor in capitalism, there is a significant difference between the thousands-of-years-old religious beliefs, compared with the 21st century doctrines of the advanced Western countries.

Some religions do not differ from capitalism in their socio-economic systems, in the sense that some are super-rich, while most religious followers are super-poor and there is no endeavour from the rich religious countries to narrow the wealth gap between them and the most impoverished worshippers in developing countries. As a simple example, compare the wealth in the Arabian Gulf with the poverty in Africa and Asia.

Some religions have become like commercial organisations, investing money in commodities. In the UK, St Paul's Cathedral charges money for even entering the church in contrast to what Jesus Christ did when he entered the temple and drove out all who were buying and selling. The temple is for prayer, not a theatre or gallery where one must pay an entrance fee.

Most religions have political extremists inciting hatred towards others and brainwashing followers to kill, terrorise and destroy others. The Muslim extremists, for example, are not even following what their Prophet Mohammed said during the Hadith 'talks' for peace builders, when he said: "If someone shows no compassion to people, God will show no compassion to him."

It is even funnier and so double standards, when Moses, over 3,200 years ago, killed the guard of Ramses II, escaped with his followers to the desert and brought the ten commandments: one of them is "Thou shalt not kill." Maybe he learned from his mistake, as we all are still learning. Ironically, it is alleged that Prophet Mohammed forbade alcohol after he got drunk one night and got up killed his friend in anger.

However, let's forget the past. Humanity evolves all the time and humans learn from their mistakes, then find restrictive measures to prevent unethical behaviour. It is disappointing that some people are afraid of change, remain living in the past and never progress to an advanced civilisation.

Perhaps, the time has come to extract the moral values and the right teachings from the old religious systems to adapt them to our modern life, merge them with our socio-economic systems and dissolve them all in one furnace to extract the new Eco-socio-economic system and become more forgiving and fairer to all humans.

Most religions say, there is only one God and yet there are many religions on the planet have different convictions of what God says or wants or is. However, let us assume that God means morality, ethics, discipline, humanity and all the right names you can give to God's decrees.

But, also, the democratic government's principles say and want the same thing and all humans on this planet need the same moral principles. In this case, we all worship the same God whether we belong to a religion or not. We must all worship the 'god of ethics' and agree on what those ethics are.

Ecolism wishes to unite the Christians, Muslims, Buddhists, Hindus, Jews and those following other religions under the banner of an Eco-religion such as Ecolism. Or at least to agree on universal moral values compatible with their religious moral ones, but which have been adapted to our modern times and principles without conflicting with international human rights and ethics.

Religions do not have to abandon the ethical teachings of their prophets if they are happy with them and should translate the old teachings to our modern life without imposing their rules on others. No matter what differences there are among various religions and traditions, there are always some common moral grounds to bring them together, living under the same banner.

Ecolism does not interfere in the doctrines of religions or any other socio-economic system but avoids their negative influences and learns from their failures to create a better Eco-socio-economic system.

Ecolism hopes that a new ethical Eco-socio-economic

system will supersede the old ones and will lead by example for future generations to come together and integrate into one social system that ensures human rights, liberties, equality, justice, peace and harmony for all humankind.

Each person's Eco-freedom ends when the Eco-freedom of others begins. Freedom is a universal consensus that comes with the responsibility for not harming yourself or others, physically, financially, morally, emotionally, religiously or influentially.

PART 5

Ecolism Socio-Economic System

The meaning of 'socio-economic system' is as it sounds: social and economic interaction with rules. Effectively, the economic factor impacts the social and vice versa. On national and international levels, the political or religious system sets the principles and regulations that dictate how people must live and interact with each other, socially and economically.

Throughout the millennia, religious systems have governed alongside the dictatorships of kings and the public has hardly had any say in influencing the laws. In recent centuries, the public's influence has risen and they have had a say in changing the laws. Hence, politicians have listened and interacted with societies to set up the principles and rules of their socio-economic system. However, it is not enough, because poverty and injustices still exist.

Just to give few examples: in a democratic system, people elect their trusted leader to set out the principles of interaction among them and when they are not happy they may choose to not elect the same leader again. But when all leaders are the same, does it matter whom the people elect?

Companies and organisations lobby leaders to change the laws to suit the rich, not the poor or the consumer. Consequently, it is not a real democratic system because capitalism compromises it. While in Ecolism's Eco-socio-economic system the leaders are transparent, are selected if they can resist the temptations of bribery by the rich and are then elected. However, leaders can be voted down and tried for misconduct. In Ecolism civil servants, politicians, solicitors and doctors have no immunity to protect them from unaccountability.

Throughout recent centuries, revolutions have changed whole political systems and principles. Nowadays, strikes and petitions might cause a policy U-turn and voting in an election removes a failing political party from power.

However, wealthy organisations still lobby the newly elected political party to do the same thing all over again and tailor laws to suit them. So, it does not matter which party is in power; the lobbyists have the real power and not the public.

Conversely, in Ecolism there are no parties, no lobbyists or powerful corporations. Each elected official is independent and judged by their success or failure.

The conclusions and facts from all the aforementioned are that no socio-economic system has so far succeeded altogether in ending poverty in the world, nor has one enforced full equality and absolute justice for everyone, creating a level playing field between the rich and poor concurrently.

Therefore, I hope that people will follow the new Eco-socio-economic system that is fairer to all or at least is fairer for the poorest in society.

The new utopian Eco-socio-economic system need not change any religion or political system but takes the most vulnerable ones in society and offers them a fairer lifestyle in an organised, visionary Eco-city with its own rules, as a large organisation would have, without conflicting with any current legal system.

PART 6

The Eco-Principles of Ecolism

Henri Maalouf declares:

In our world of complexity and diversity, we have over regulated and over legislated imperfect laws that serve the rich more than the poor.

The current laws in the Western socio-economic systems are written in vague and complicated ways that lead to various interpretations. These cumbersome laws and rules hardly have any clear yes or no answers or define interpretations as it is given in the Oxford dictionary. It is normally up to a judge to interpret laws and deduce the relevant one to a case out of the myriad of other conflicting ones to reach a judgment. It is like a piece of rubber stretched by the handler. It is like politicians who never answer a question directly.

The proposed Eco-socio-economic system does not need myriad of complicated laws full of loopholes. Instead, it trusts a conscious Eco-judge to make decrees in accordance with the purpose of the law and its ethical principles, not its literal and varied interpretations.

The subsequent sections of this part of the book are the

guidelines for an Eco-judge to legislate and make the law from simple Eco-principles to protect the interests of everyone equally.

The details of the Eco-principles are beyond the remit of this book and will be detailed further in the next Ecolism volume. What is categorised here is a starting point for guidance to the Eco-judges to refine and complete.

Principles and rules get amended all the time, building on experience and lack of foresight about what might happen in the future. The world is full of laws and, most of the time, they become bureaucratic, cumbersome, vague, not decisive and unfair to some more than others.

Most laws are influenced by lobbyists to suit their vested interests at the expense of the public. Sometimes, the regulations limit people's freedom, invade privacy and deprive us of our human rights.

The challenge is to learn from all the legislative systems and extract their relevant abstracts, then adapt them to the Eco-lifestyle and Eco-principles. The Eco-principles should be more of a 'moral common sense and macro conceptualism' context, rather than detailed clauses for various circumstances and the variations of penalties for subtle differences in offences.

It does not matter whether a crime is big or small, financial penalty or imprisonment is not enough and is not the absolute solution. Instead, a proper re-education programme must be implemented to reform the offender and prevent the offence from reoccurring.

In any case, the following categories are the most commonly used ones and the objective of each is described to guide Eco-judges and subject-matter experts in writing the relevant principles for the right disciplinary actions, deterrents and reform solutions to avoid offences reoccurring. The Eco-judge assesses the financial consequences, psychiatrists recommend the rehabilitation programmes and the administration proposes the changes required for the systems.

The following is a flavour of the guidelines for the most critical issues. It is up to the Eco-judges, lawyers, psychologists, philosophers and administrators to set out the principles and rules. The Eco-city's laws are written as a social charter, equivalent to a country's constitution, but should not conflict with national laws.

Eco-Freedom Principle

The responsible Eco-freedom is the mother of all principles. Eco-freedom means people can do anything they like if they do not harm themselves or others. This includes harm caused financially, physically, mentally, socially, influentially or spiritually and by any other form that upsets the balance of freedoms' equalities. And, as the saying goes: "your freedom ends where the freedom of others begins".

Eco-freedom is the highest principle in the Eco-city and Ecolism overrules any other policy or rule. Its definition in the Eco-city is responsible freedom, where no one should limit the freedom of others, as long as he or she do not harm themselves or anyone else in any ethical circumstance. The majority determines the Eco-freedom limitations and overrides any other rule or individual's vested interests in any business or personal gain.

The will of the majority overrides the will of the minority and this is what democracy is all about. But if an amendment to an Eco-principle satisfies both the majority and minority, then it is a preferable option. Otherwise, the minorities should adapt and integrate or leave and migrate.

Eco-freedom in Ecolism does not interfere with any other principles or religions. It gives its Eco-society the responsible freedom to choose their way of life. After the majority decide on a particular lifestyle, it becomes a constitution that is not easy to change. However, if circumstances change, then it is logical to adapt and request another majority vote for the amendments.

The Eco-justice inside the Eco-city complies with the external national laws; however, internally, people can freely follow ethical practices. In other words, you can apply your own rules to your own house as long as you do not harm yourself or others or force your children or spouse to follow unreasonable or unacceptable rules.

For example, let us consider a scenario: the father has high cholesterol or diabetes and eats particular foods such as fish, vegetables and salads and cannot eat sweets or fatty food, while the mother is a meat eater and can tolerate all the fat and desserts, but does not eat vegetables or salads. Then, the son is omnivorous and can eat any food, but the daughter is a pure vegetarian or vegan. In this case, the father should not force them to eat according to his diet, but he cannot afford to buy caviar and champagne for them. Therefore, each can eat what he or she likes, but within the limitation of the available budget and should eat what harms none of them.

Although the principle of freedom includes free speech, it does not mean allowing irresponsible speech that incites hatred, causes harm to others and disturbs the peace. Expressing views must not be misleading, like what some politicians say or encourage people to go on strike, causing economic loss to others.

However, people should be able to petition and remove from unfair power rulers, unscrupulous employers and anyone that abuses their authority to limit people's freedom, which results in an injustice. In a nutshell, authorities' intervention to restrict freedoms is valid when people step outside the responsible Eco-freedom lines or principles.

As another example of responsible freedom, financial institutions are not free to charge interest at any amount they see fit for the criteria they create. Corporations make salaries a big secret to hide their inequality and dictate their unfair terms, which is to make more profits or protect the rich more than the poor. This is not responsible freedom.

In this scenario, the government must intervene and limit the financial institutions or companies' irresponsible use of freedom by dictating their terms. Salaries should be known and transparent and the charges should be limited. Similar rules apply to everything people do to ensure equality, real justice and harmonious, peaceful societies.

Eco-Human-Rights Principle

The minimum Eco-human right for each Ecolist is to be cared for from the cradle to the grave and receive the full benefits of the Eco-welfare system, which means free Eco-education and skills training for life, Eco-healthcare, an Eco-home, an Eco-lifestyle, free access to the Eco-city's front-line services and Eco-justice. But the Ecolists also have an obligation to work and pay taxes to cover the cost of the Eco-welfare benefits system, abide by the Eco-City's Eco-Magna-Carta and Eco-principles and be good, ethical citizens.

Note: In *Ecolism 3*, there is a complete section about human rights, which re-writes the existing ones and adds to them.

Eco-Equality Principle

Whether someone is a woman or man, an adult or child, a person of any race or colour, rich or poor, able-bodied or disabled, a person in authority or not, everyone is equal, independent, responsibly free and to be treated like any other, but rewarded on their merits, efforts and ethical endeavours.

The new Eco-socio-economic system creates a classless society, where everyone is equal, but some will reap more rewards than others, depending on his or her efforts, qualifications and merits, which is to encourage people to work harder and smarter to earn more. The more they give to their Eco-socio-economic system, the more they get out of it, in predetermined and proportionate structural ways.

Eco-Administration Principle

Transparency is the essential principle for the Eco-administration. Every conversation, document and email must be recorded and monitored against the ethical code of conduct. Failure to file every action leads to a suspicion of misconduct and wrongdoing. Efficiency and good value for money are vital parts of the processes in any administration. Furthermore, wasting taxpayers' money and valuable resources becomes an offence.

Failure to deliver promised manifestos, reform programmes, an adequate welfare system or employment for everyone would result in a call for a vote of no confidence and replacement with more successful administrators. Rewards for success can be given only on improving the existing Eco-welfare system. Adversely, failure to improve the welfare system opens doors for a vote of no confidence and dismissal without rewards or compensation.

Administrators or people in authority should not have privileged immunity; they are accountable for their actions like any other person and can be tried for any failure or misconduct. They must abide by all other Eco-principles, with no exceptions, to enforce equality.

Eco-Truth Principle

If we have done nothing wrong, not lied or hidden the truth, then there is nothing to fear from being transparent and telling the truth. But knowing what others do is sometimes knowledge that can be abused and then the abusers must be removed from and deprived of that knowledge.

For example, the NSA (National Security Agency in the USA) and GCHQ (Government Communications Headquarters in the UK) have the right to monitor and know about the activities of every citizen and this knowledge is the power that can be used against each citizen. In this case, that right should not exist if it is abused.

Therefore, knowing the truth is a double-edged sword, which can be wielded either for or against each party. If an edge of the sword is used for unethical conduct by the holder, then it must be removed. In any case, nothing justifies hiding the truth with all of its consequences and nothing justifies the misuse of the sword of justice.

If what we have is rightfully ours, then no one should take our rights from us, unless we abuse the use of our rights. Speaking the truth without misleading others is an ethical and civilised virtue that everyone must abide by and do. The truth sometimes hurts, but a lie hurts much more. As the shortest route between two points is a straight line, the fact is that the shortest path to progress and human wellbeing is the truth.

In Ecolism, speaking the truth is a way of life and hiding it, lying or being misleading is an Eco-offence, which leads to a trial, rehabilitation and paying for the damage caused by lying.

In our 21st century, misleading others, avoiding telling the truth or only telling part of it, accusing others without proof and the wrong interpretation of words and actions are becoming so common that people think it is the modern way of living and the norm. Maybe our civilisation needs another Messiah to tell humanity that the divine rule is telling the truth, the whole truth and nothing but the truth. Any deviation from the truth is a sinful act that must be punished or the person reformed and this rule includes politicians and business.

Eco-Justice Principle

Eco-justice in Ecolism justly rewards success and effort, reforms failure, eliminates poverty, equalises the inequalities between the layers of society and ensures that everyone is treated the same regardless of his or her wealth, influence or social status.

Removing the cause of an action prevents its effects and occurrence. Therefore, the Eco-judge's orders will not be imprisonment and financial penalties, but rather reform and rehabilitation after finding the root causes of the offences.

Imprisonment creates more hatred and a sense of revenge and does not remove the genetic factors that caused the offence, the psychological effects of the social circumstances nor any root cause. It is usually a flaw in a socio-economic system that must be reformed to prevent such re-occurrences.

A financial penalty is not a deterrent either, especially for the wealthy who can afford such judgments. However, if it is a major crime causing financial losses to others or misconduct for personal gains, then it adds up to the rehabilitation, reform and isolation.

If all the above fails, the final judgment by the Eco-supreme-judge is expulsion from the Eco-city after exhausting all other disciplinary measures.

Eco-Tort Principles

This principle is about any wrongful or non-ethical act that results in causing harm to others, including non-compliance, overcharging, misleading, withholding information, stealing, bribery, misconduct, abusing authority or anything that infringes on people's Eco-freedom.

The penalty is usually re-education and temporary isolation in reform centres, but other financial losses should be paid back twofold as a deterrent to stop the person from doing it again.

Eco-Sexual-Assault Principle

Sexual assault is an important category within the Eco-tort principle and is taken very seriously. Naturally, in an Eco-city, people are free to have sex with each other anytime they like, with whom they like, but only after mutual agreement.

Aggressive non-consensual sex is a crime, paying money for sex is also a crime, as is any form of influence, blackmail, bargaining exchange or using drugs to force the other person to surrender to having sex. However, occasional and non-aggressive gentle forcible sex between partners could be tolerated a little as part of an agreement; otherwise, separation becomes necessary upon repetition.

The penalty is re-education, isolation and public naming and shaming, in addition to a substantial financial fine. Paedophiles are extreme sexual offenders and need prolonged psychological treatment or expulsion from the Eco-city.

Eco-Criminal Principle

Killing and causing grievous bodily harm are absolute offensive crimes, which require immediate isolation, severe long-term re-education and the financial penalty of paying the victim all the offender's income for life.

Accidental killing is still considered dangerous negligence punishable by rehabilitation and a monetary penalty decided by the Eco-judge. Killing might require surrendering the murderer to the national courts for further prosecution and permanent expulsion from the Eco-city.

Eco-Environment Principle

The Eco-environment principle asserts there should be 0% pollution in the Eco-city. Hence, any non-compliance from anybody is a serious Eco-tort offence and the security teams will bring the offender's activities to an immediate halt. Licensing of any industry or products should have strict conditions for compliance with the Eco-environment principle.

Eco-Business Licensing

Licensing and accepting a business or industry to operate in the Eco-city depends on the business or industry accepting the Eco-code-of-conduct, complying with the Eco-principles and their compatibility with the Eco-city's Eco-socio-economic system.

The main criterion for acceptance is not using or producing any pollutants of the environment, such as fossil fuels (e.g. coal, petroleum or other materials that create more than 0% of carbon dioxide [CO_2], nitrous oxide [N_2O] and other harmful gas emissions).

No harmful chemicals or plastics are allowed and the crops should not be exposed to insecticides or have any genetic modifications. If metal can be replaced by more Eco-friendly materials such as wood, fibreglass or other recyclable materials, it may become compulsory not to use metals. The products available for use inside the Eco-city should be one of the materials on the Eco-city's white list, which is an acceptable Eco-product.

Certain businesses or products can be allowed to be exported or sold outside the Eco-city. Gambling, betting and unlicensed lotteries or charity lotteries shall not be allowed to operate inside the Eco-city in any shape or form. Lending money to small businesses or individuals is via the commercial bank at a reasonable interest rate only. And the list of Eco-licensing for Eco-businesses will continue to grow in this direction under the Eco-concept.

Eco-Business' Principles

The Eco-judges, Eco-councillors, Eco-businesses, Eco-industry and Eco-agriculture committees, in addition to the Eco-workforce committee, will meet and write the Eco-business principles that are agreed by all parties.

Commercial principles can be complicated, but in the Eco-city it will be made simple and standardised and it will apply to everyone, but there are a few exceptions, depending on the nature of the business. For example, one Eco-business principle allows 5% tax-free profits for turnover in millions, but the traders and the commercial banks might have a turnover of billions. Therefore, a different rule applies and the tax-free percentage might be much lower.

The following is a starting point and the administration will add much more detail. However, the details should not be too complicated or vague and should have no loopholes. The Eco-principles should balance the rights of the investors and the employees in the Eco-city simultaneously.

Eco-Business Principle 1: Any business, agriculture or industry that operates in the Eco-city's zones must be licensed by the Eco-city, have the Eco-prefix added to its name and work independently from its parent company. It must have its own independent budget, a local profit and loss account and pay taxes on any sales in the Eco-city, after deducting the agreed expenditure.

Eco-Business Principle 2: If the profits of a business drop below 5% or the allowed tax-free margin, it would be considered to be a non-profitable business unable to pay taxes. Therefore, it must restructure, change management or ownership, the workforce must take over or move to a more successful business.

Eco-Business Principle 3: The Eco-city-commercial-bank, in cooperation with the Eco-tax-inspectors, will continuously monitor businesses for profitability and try to help with resolving issues, reducing overhead expenditure and finding export markets.

Note: It is in the best interest of the Eco-city that the business makes reasonable profits to pay more taxes and employ more Ecolists; therefore, the Eco-finance-councillor intervenes upon the failure to make a profit and pay taxes.

Eco-Business Principle 4: The allowed expenditure must be limited and any excessive or extravagant advertising or spending must be agreed upon and justified. The expenses allowed for tax purposes should be limited; for example, Eco-workforce costs, machines, equipment, Eco-furniture and raw or imported materials from cheaper and accepted international sources, besides many others.

The following also can be considered for tax exemption purposes: Eco-electricity, which is free, but it has an investment cost; the premises, which are free or leased at a reasonable rate; the building's investment cost; and so on. A realistic list of exemptions can be composed.

Any non-standard expenditure must be approved by the Eco-committees and the Eco-tax inspectors to ensure that the business remains profitable and pays the required taxes.

Eco-Business Principle 5: Eco-security will monitor the businesses' management for transparency, the Eco-workforce for productivity, the specialists' integrity and any possible sabotage or revealing business secrets to competitors. The Eco-workforce must sign a non-disclosure agreement not to talk or write about work outside the workplace.

Eco-Business Principle 6: The Eco-ICT-data-centre is the sole provider of information technology (IT) solutions and requirements for all businesses with no exceptions. The Eco-ICT will ensure security and maximum performance for communications.

Eco-Business Principle 7: The Eco-sales-force and Eco-call-centres, including those who work from home in the Eco-city, are the only sales and service force for the Eco-businesses and dedicated teams are trained in each business to understand and sell or service their products.

Eco-Business Principle 8: The Eco-city-commercial-bank is the only bank allowed to be used for business transactions (sales and expenditure in the Eco-city). Each business must have an Eco-account for the Eco-business in the Eco-city-commercial-bank and taxes can be reserved and deducted at source from this account.

Eco-Business Principle 9: All businesses must abide by the Eco-city's covenants and principles and comply with its Eco-socio-economic system.

Eco-Business Principle 10: The Eco-businesses will pay an agreed hourly rate to the employees in the Eco-workforce and no one is allowed to strike or stop production. The committees agree on the principles that sustain the interests of the Eco-city above all other interests.

Eco-Industry Principles

The Eco-industry principles are the same as the Eco-business principles, except for some specific ones that apply to industries only. It could be different agreed expenditures, patents and intellectual property rights' costs, in conjunction with the Eco-research-and-innovation-centre.

Eco-Intellectual-Property Principle

The Eco-city's research-and-innovation centre is universal and accepts people from all around the world. The innovations and inventions are the intellectual property of the initiator, with a percentage paid to the Eco-city for providing the facilities and free accommodation. Companies and industries might charge for feasibility and validity studies for research and agree on a proportion of the royalties being paid to the initiator or owner of the invention or the research value.

Ecolism considers that it is unfair if a company employs someone to invent new products and pays them a regular salary, preserving the intellectual property rights, unless it is a simple improvement on a patented invention. The inventor should be compensated generously for the design and paid an acceptable amount of money to relinquish their copyright. Rewarding the inventors coming to the Eco-city will encourage them to work in the Eco-research-and-innovation-centre.

Eco-Agriculture Principles

The Eco-agriculture principles for ethical conduct are similar to the Eco-business and Eco-industrial principles. However, agriculture must not use pesticides or insecticides and must find alternatives to protect the crops. Also, they must not genetically modify food; all the agriculture must be naturally grown or catalysed with temperature-controlled enclosures and natural fertilisers.

A sample of each organically grown food batch must be tested in the lab and labelled for the actual nutritional values, not given standard labels printed off a computer program. The farms must endeavour to produce the most nutritious food needed by the Eco-city and recommended by the Eco-nutritionists.

The farmers should also grow medicinal herbs and extract the active and useful ingredients from them, in natural ways, to help to cure minor ailments. The agriculture will supply the Eco-city with food first, then export the excess.

Eco-Contracts-and-Agreements Principle

Eco-agreements are standard Eco-city templates issued by Eco-justice and verified by the Eco-court before being signed by both parties to avoid future disputes. The contract's terms and conditions protect the interests of both the supplier and the consumer in a balanced way. Agreements can be terminated at any time the service is no longer required or if the vendor fails to deliver. The terms must be simple, readable, clear and easily understood. The contracts between the Eco-city and businesses are binding and any dispute is resolved in the Eco-courts of the Eco-city only.

Eco-Dispute Principle

The Eco-justice in the Eco-city is the only court for any disputes and it is up to the Eco-supreme-judge to transfer a case to the national jurisdiction if required. The international laws do not apply or interfere in the Eco-city's legislation or principles. However, if a dispute or an incident happens outside the Eco-city, then the relevant jurisdiction applies.

Eco-Property-and-Equity Principle

The Eco-properties or Eco-equities are transferable inside the Eco-city. Each person takes their investment with them when they change Eco-homes, as individual assets. For example, if two partners paid a different repayment amount of money on an Eco-home, each takes with him/her what he/she paid. No one is allowed to sell an Eco-home to anyone outside the Eco-city. The Eco-city will buy any equity or Eco-home to sell to selected people permitted to enter the Eco-city.

Similarly, the businesses and industries also offer the Eco-city the first refusal to purchase a failing business or industry. And it is up to the Eco-administration to accept a new owner for any company to ensure their compliance with the Eco-city's rules. Otherwise, the company shuts down and comes under the receivership of the Eco-city or the Ecolists might run the company and try to make it profitable or move to a more successful business.

Eco-Covenant Principle

If three build it, then three share it and no one is better than the other because, without any one of the three, the rest could not complete it. However, the shares should reflect the amount of contribution of each.

An Eco-covenant is an agreement between the Ecolists and the tripartite administration, which means the investors, the workforce and the elected councillors.

Although the Eco-council provides an Eco-home for each couple on relaxed terms, it will be conditional in the Eco-covenant that they can be removed from the Eco-city without compensation at any time if they violate the Eco-city's principles or the Eco-Magna-Carta, as would happen when signing a contract where terms and conditions apply.

This way, there is much to lose and the residents will

be hesitant to offend or be unwilling to work when offered a reasonable opportunity or retraining in new skills, especially when there is a commitment to pay the mortgage on their Eco-homes. In other words, work for it or lose it.

PART 7

Eco-Magna-Carta

The Eco-socio-economic system in Ecolism can be applied anywhere; however, in a case where there is a conflict with national laws and it becomes forbidden, then an internal Eco-Magna-Carta or Eco-social-charter can be applied in an Eco-city or town. What you can do in your house, does not need the neighbours' interference as long as you do not harm yourself and your family. Therefore, the Eco-Magna-Carta is merely an agreement between a group of people, businesses and the administration inside an Eco-city. It is similar to a conglomerate's internal rules or a university's social charter.

The Eco-City's Eco-Magna-Carta is its internal Eco-socio-economic system designed for a sustainable, self-sufficient and harmonious Eco-lifestyle, abiding by its Eco-principles, to present decent living for everyone as a compulsory human right.

The Eco-Magna-Carta's guidelines and Eco-principles are basic common sense and an agreement between the authorities, businesses and the public as a troika or tripartite system of governance, with each party having equal powers, to ensure fairness for the people and protection for the investors, while disciplined by its elected rulers.

The Eco-Magna-Carta outlines the primary set of Eco-principles as philosophical and ethical guidance for governing the Eco-city, complemented by standardised templates for Eco-rules that do not contradict human rights, equalities or Eco-responsible-freedom.

Building an Eco-city or town as a physical structure is not sufficient to make the necessary social changes to an unfair socio-economic system unless we reform or replace it with a better Eco-socio-economic system.

The primary objective of the Eco-Magna-Carta is to create the social principles for the Eco-city and the Eco-society that do not conflict with national laws and to ensure equality, justice and survival regardless of any global economic turmoil.

The Eco-principles and rules proposed in this book will need lawyers, academics, the public, Eco-councillors, businesses and judges to work out the details without overriding the purposes of the principles. The public has the final say and must vote, using the Eco-city's website, on any changes to the principles. Once the majority agrees on the final version or draft of the principles, then they must abide by them as a covenant and binding agreement and become subject to its consequences for non-compliance.

The Eco-city's Eco-Magna-Carta applies zero tolerance to non-compliance with its principles and rules. However, the Eco-Magna-Carta is based on prevention rather than cure and reformation or rehabilitation rather than penalties.

The aim is to create an Eco-society's Eco-Magna-Carta that has a social-economic system that ensures the overall Eco-social welfare for a progressive Eco-lifestyle that is self-sufficient and sustainable. The aim also includes the political, industrial, agricultural and commercial systems to ensure the harmony of coexistence in a stable human ecosystem.

The fundamental principles and philosophy of the Eco-

Magna-Carta are to give people the final say on which rules to follow and which representatives they may trust to organise their lifestyle or their wellbeing.

It is always a question of who guards the guard guarding my gold? In the Eco-socio-economic system of the Eco-city, it is not the Eco-finance-councillor, the Eco-mayor, the Eco-supreme-judge or all the councillors combined, including the committees and all the administrators, who have the authority and final word. The Ecolists only have the absolute power and decide on which infrastructure is suitable for them or which principles and rules apply to them.

Giving power to the people is a democracy. The majority vote always decides and has the final say on appointing the guardians of their gold. The vote of the majority must not be overturned to suit the minority or the vested interests of the elite few.

In the Eco-socio-economic system, it is an irrevocable Eco-principle to give people the power to decide how they wish to live. However, the experts and specialists know better and it is their duty to prove and explain in layman's terms the validity of their advice and proposals.

The major decisions are a synergetic interaction between the governors and the governed. It should be based on the majority vote with no influence placed on people to vote one way or the other. The voters should not be given misleading information or a limited choice of two parties or candidates only. People should be able to say no to both candidates or say none of the above.

The Eco-principles evolve to set out the main rules that govern the Eco-councillors, businesses and the public to maintain an eternal status quo, with beneficial and fairer collaboration among them. The majority must agree on each Eco-principle and make it a constitutional lifetime commandment that cannot be changed, amended, added to or removed unless most of the Ecolists vote to approve it.

The Eco-principles must be concise, well defined and easy to read and understand with no vagueness or different interpretations for its meanings or contexts and no principle should contradict any other or have exploitable loopholes. Any loophole should be immediately closed and notification must be given to the public for them to react to or ignore.

The Eco-principles are the parents and references that override any rule. The Eco-supreme-judge can decree its interpretation with the help of other Eco-judges and may purposely rule on cases in exceptional circumstances not covered by the Eco-principles. The precedents of the exceptions should not replace the principles or be easily used for similar situations.

There will be three levels of court: level one for minor disputes and the offences of individuals, level two for more-severe ones and level three for collective conflicts between the public and the tripartite government. The Eco-supreme-judge can overrule all levels and the last call is for a resolution by the Eco-mayor or the public's majority vote.

The Eco-judge of each court is assisted by solicitors, psychologists, security personnel and subject-matter experts to extract the truth from both the claimant and the defendant. In an Eco-city, the solicitor does not defend any applicant, but investigates all allegations from all parties involved.

The Eco-judges decree the rehabilitation of offenders or their removal from the Eco-city; and propose changes to the Eco-socio-economic system and the Eco-principles or rules, to prevent the reoccurrence of offences. Also, they may request the creation of solutions to eliminate the root causes of the problems.

The solicitors represent neither the defendant nor the

claimant. They are both interrogated and questioned until the truth comes out. The Eco-judge or prosecution can use any compelling, civilised methods to extract the truth without influencing the subject to admit to anything other than the facts.

The Eco-Magna-Carta is the collection of all approved Eco-principles for the Eco-socio-economic system as a codified constitution that cannot be changed easily without the approval of the majority and no objections from the minorities.

All the judges, solicitors, councillors and subject-matter experts can propose to the Eco-supreme-judge the necessary changes to the Eco-principles and rules, but the public must vote to approve such changes.

The Eco-principles for the Eco-socio-economic system are the philosophical guidance and starting points for the Ecolists, subject-matter experts and Eco-judges to consider and legislate accordingly, helped by the Eco-councillors.

PART 8

The Human Ecosystem of Ecolism

By definition, an ecosystem is a biological community of interacting organisms and their physical environment. In my concept, the human ecosystem means people interacting with their physical and socio-economic environments.

However, the whole planet is an ecosystem of various sub-ecosystems and so is the universe. Each sub-ecosystem interacts with others and any imbalance in one affects the others.

For example, each forest; each colony of bees, ants, birds or insects; and each group of animals have their own ecosystems. And each of their ecosystems becomes a sub-ecosystem of a greater, encircling ecosystem, designed by the planet or universe, including the human sub-ecosystem. So, in short, imagine the world is one great ecosystem 'like God' and each small ecosystem is a subsystem of the greater one. Hence, the integrity of the smaller ones stabilises the balance of the vast ecosystem.

Each ecosystem has its own community that interacts with its environment to sustain and recycle its existence. However, the human activities sometimes act in ways that affect most other ecosystems and upset the balance of the planet's ecosystem. Therefore, the human form of organism, which has the highest intelligence, must learn that destroying other ecosystems will affect the whole planetary one and that people need its integrity to survive longer and live better.

The Ecolism series of books are specifically written to help people understand how to create a human ecosystem that does not destroy the other ones on the planet.

The philosophy of Ecolism explains to people how to preserve the natural habitat and the environment, i.e. other ecosystems. This includes wars that kill people and animals. In a nutshell, people should not pollute the environment around them whether it is the land, air or sea.

We must learn from nature and compare and observe how other ecosystems work. It is a perfect creation, whether we believe that it was designed by an invisible God or by an invisible cosmic force of repetitive cycles of big bangs. Humans evolved to live in a little tiny shell inside colossal layers of universal envelopes. We are a minuscule component of a grander design of nature and we can never create a better one. Hence, we must understand the natural ecosystems of the planet, learn and adapt to conform to its inherent design, simply because it is beyond our ability to invent better planetary ecosystems.

I like to compare the human ecosystem with the bees living in their ecosystem as a colony in a hive. The drones (male bees) fertilise their queen who lays eggs that undergo a complete metamorphosis (many stages of change) to become adult worker bees (female bees making honey, serving the colony and pollinating the plants in the outside world, in addition to producing honey in the hive).

Eventually, the queen, after serving her purpose, swarms away (leaving with most of the bees to build another colony in another hive), giving way for the new queen to continue the lifecycle of the bees' ecosystem.

The human ecosystem, in comparison, is where a community of people live in shelters, serving as a country or a city and interacting with the rest of the world.

Typically, a society elects a leader, then a group of representatives (members of parliament or senators), create an excellent socio-economic system for the society that helps people to propagate, reproduce, work and nurture the children to grow and become adults, who will eventually do the same after the older ones die. And, in time, the elected leader leaves, giving way to someone else to serve and continue the human ecosystem's lifecycle.

However, the current global socio-economic systems have unbalanced import/export deficits. There is dominance of one over another and the reliance of one country on another. This is unlike the concept of the utopian Eco-city, where I propose an Eco-socio-economic system that ensures self-sufficiency.

In my opinion, the current trends in the socio-economic systems of our civilisation are slowly destroying the planet's environment and the human ecosystem and will shorten the planet's lifespan. Moreover, countries create wars to kill each other, mostly for dominance and as a result of the economic greed of the most powerful. This trend must be reversed and should not continue; instead, it must be replaced by new Eco-socio-economic systems that last forever.

It is like the evolution of Homo Erectus to Homo Sapiens; we must evolve further to become Eco-humans living in a peaceful and sustainable human ecosystem.

We cannot become Eco-humans if we live as predators and prey, with the stronger killing the weaker to feed upon or dominate them or the richer forcibly snatching the wealth from the poorer to satisfy their human greed and selfishness. Consequently, as long as we fight each other – physically, financially and for domination – we are not civilised enough to become Eco-humans.

For the Eco-society in my utopian Eco-city, living in an Eco-socio-economic system is the first step in evolving into a better human species and becoming Eco-humans, residing in communities that are human Eco-hives peacefully surviving self-sufficiently from the available surroundings to preserve the planet's ecosystem.

Ecolism 2 talks about building an Eco-city. It can be done by any developer or government. However, even if it is made to reduce the CO_2, N_2O, CH_4 and other chemical pollutants to 0%, it solves half the problem. The other half can be solved by creating ethical Eco-governance that ensures the wellbeing of its inhabitants.

PART 1

Eco-Governance

This section sets up guidelines for the governance of an Eco-city, based on an Eco-socio-economic system. It is up to the Ecolists, businesses and Eco-councillors' committees and the Eco-administration to work out the details and amend them as deems to be necessary for a design of an Eco-city.

The Eco-governance includes three governing committees, the Eco-mayor and the Eco-supreme-judge. The governing committees are the Eco-councillor, Eco-business and Ecolist committees. Each one of them has equal powers to the others; they govern as a tripartite system and run the Eco-city as a conglomerate runs a global enterprise, with its internal rules and as outlined in all aspects of Ecolism and its Eco-socio-economic system. The Eco-supreme-judge and the Eco-mayor have the last say in disputes and can remove anyone who abuses authority, defies Eco-principles or causes harm to the wellbeing of the Ecolists.

The following are the major elements of the Eco-governance:

The members of the Eco-councillor committee are the governors of the Eco-city who are responsible for enforcing compliance with the Eco-principles and the wellbeing of the Ecolists. They are supported by Eco-administrators to run the Eco-front-line-services for the Eco-city.

The Eco-business committee is formed from representatives of the industries, businesses and agriculture. The Eco-business committee ensures compliance with the Eco-city's rules and collaborates with the other two committees to resolve issues and avoid conflicts for the mutual benefits of all. The Eco-business committee can create its own rules for the selection and election of its members.

The Ecolist committee is elected by the Ecolists who are the inhabitants of the Eco-city or a community in the case of a town. Their responsibility is to ensure no applied Eco-principles or new rules negatively impact the wellbeing of the Ecolists.

The Eco-supreme-judge has the final say in interpreting the purposes of the Eco-principles and the fairness of the Eco-socio-economic system. The Eco-supreme-judge has the power to remove any person in authority including Eco-councillors, companies' CEOs or anyone who endangers the wellbeing of the Ecolists and the progress of the Eco-city.

The Eco-mayor of the Eco-city has the final word in deciding on the direction and philosophy of the Eco-socio-economic system. Also, he/she represents the Eco-city globally and can remove anyone in power who may cause any harm to the Ecolists, including the Eco-supreme-judge. He/she has the authority to dissolve any major dispute between any parties inside and outside the Eco-city.

The election voting process is more efficient and economical and the results are immediate. Ecolists older than 16 browse the Eco-city's website from their Eco-home and select the dedicated menu for voting. Then, they log in with a two-step verification password, the system takes a facial picture and the election form asks for ID and an address to verify the voter. The system then presents the choice of candidates for the election. The electronic or internet-based

Eco-voting system is designed to allow eligible persons to vote only once.

The following part outlines the guidelines for the Eco-governors to work out the details for the Eco-socio-economic system. There should be some sort of governance system and rules before building an Eco-city. Once it is built, then more details or amendments might be necessary as needs arise and circumstances change.

The Eco-mayor

The Eco-mayor acts like a field marshal of an army, with executive powers in a battle and has many generals helping in various areas. However, the field marshal might have climbed the ladder from being a soldier, stepping upon each step through the ranks to become a field marshal eventually.

The Eco-mayor must have a good education, multiple skills and experiences, a philosophical mind and an ethical mentality to qualify for selection before being elected.

It is vital that the Eco-mayor is chosen by the public and not appointed by a political party or a group of business lobbyists, nor by the Eco-councillors or the Eco-supreme-judge. As a matter of fact, the Eco-mayor must be impartial, independent and must not belong to any organisation in any shape or form.

The role of the Eco-mayor is merely to act as an arbitrator or an oracle for guidance. However, he/she has the final say in major disputes or areas of indecision among the three branches of the tripartite system. Also, is the voice of the Ecolists that overrides any governance decisions.

The election of the Eco-mayor is a democratic exercise of voting by the majority of the Ecolists.

The Eco-supreme-judge

The Eco-supreme-judge is selected by all members of the Eco-justice system (the tripartite committees) and elected by the Ecolists. The Ecolists have the final say whether he/she goes or stay at any time they feel justice is not serving them.

The Eco-supreme-judge is the final authority for appealing against any judgment in the Eco-city and can refer any matter to national or international laws. But he/she also is subject to scrutiny for misconduct or biased judgments. Above all, he/she must ensure that the Ecolists are treated fairly by the Eco-welfare system, the Eco-city's employers and any policy or law applied. Any new law must be approved by the Eco-mayor, the Eco-supreme-judge and the Ecolists.

The Eco-Councillors

The Eco-councillors work together and have equal powers or responsibilities and equal votes on policies or budgets for any front-line service or project in the Eco-city. Every Eco-councillor has equal power to the others, to keep the right balance and integrity of the Eco-city's ecosystem. They all act like King Arthur's Knights of the Round Table, as each has the same power or an equal vote.

In other words, all the Eco-councillors and the selected committees work together to sustain the Eco-city's revenue, balanced with spending on the Ecolists' wellbeing from the cradle to the grave.

The Eco-councillors are answerable to the public and comply with the Eco-transparency principles, which means all their meetings and conversations should be recorded and uploaded to the Eco-city's website for the Ecolists to watch their activities and decisions on policies.

As for the characteristics and job description of an Eco-councillor, the person should be dedicated, well educated, ethical, transparent and a subject-matter expert in the service. This role is a full-time paid job. Critically, he/she should have no secondary job or vested interests in promoting any other business.

The Eco-councillor will receive a generous salary, which is more than any CEO of a business or industry in the Eco-city, plus a bonus on high performance or better delivery than promised or expected. But the Eco-councillor is highly punishable for misconduct, which is considered to be a serious offence that results in asset seizure, rehabilitation and naming and shaming, including the prohibition of running for a similar public job ever again.

The generous salary will help the Eco-councillor to relinquish any vested interests in any business or receiving a contribution from any lobbying group.

The Eco-security monitors the Eco-committees, administrators, businesses' CEOs and others for misconduct, to prevent it happening before further damage occurs. As the saying goes, prevention rather than cure is best practice. The dedicated Eco-security personnel can bring any person to trial if there is sufficient evidence, proof of misconduct or non-compliance with the purposes of the Eco-principles.

The number of specialised Eco-councillors running various divisions depends on the Eco-city's needs and services. In some circumstances, services might be consolidated together or split into more branches. The Eco-committees act as if they are branches of one tree that grow as the surrounding environment allows.

The head of the Eco-councillors is the Eco-mayor, who will settle conflicts and provide guidelines for the Eco-philosophy of the Eco-socio-economic system. However, the legality and interpretation of the Eco-principles or policies are up to the Eco-supreme-judge to finalise.

The Eco-council will directly manage the Eco-city with selected committees from businesses and public representatives. The management type is similar to a regulated, ethical and accountable organisation or a successful conglomerate organising the lives of three to four million people into a large working family.

The rationale behind running the Eco-city as a successful business with a three-pillar administration or tripartite system is because governments fail to keep nationalised services running and resort to privatisation, while enterprises succeed in running the same functions and make profits, but sometimes become unfair to the consumer. Therefore, the joined tripartite governance is the best choice.

Most humans are not yet civilised enough to be self-disciplined or self-regulated and are not sufficiently ethical. Therefore, in any governance system, the disciplinary and regulatory body is essential. We know from daily experience that most businesses put profits before ethics. Thus, the balance of 33% power for each of the three branches of the tripartite governance is essential, with a fourth to monitor and resolve deadlocks. Here, the fourth power is the Eco-mayor and the Eco-supreme-judge.

PART 2

Eco-Committees

Eco-Business Committee

The Eco-business committee has its internal rules of selecting candidates from various businesses in the Eco-industries, Eco-agriculture, Eco-commercial and Eco-small-businesses.

Ecolists Committee

The Ecolists committee has the same criteria of election as the Eco-councillors committee. It is designed to represent the Ecolists rights in employment, Eco-welfare system, equalities, freedom and all aspects of the Eco-socio-economic system that affect the wellbeing of the Ecolists.

Eco-Administration

The following sections briefly set the primary responsibilities of each proposed Eco-councillor and the Eco-city's administration. Eventually, they will set up the standards, rules and the required self-sufficiency and sustainability of the Eco-socio-economic system. Although there are various departments for different functions, all interacting with each other, but, at a high level, there are three groups or aggregations.

The first is Eco-welfare or front-line services, which includes health, education, unemployment, justice, housing and any other department that deals with the wellbeing of the Ecolists.

The second is Eco-services, which includes transport, energy, water, ICT, entertainment and communication.

The third is Eco-production, which includes industries, businesses, agriculture, employment and finance. The grouping is just to identify the costs of the first and second, which are to be balanced by the income from the third group. The endeavour is to make the first group free and the second semi-free or means tested for affordability, but the third is the group that generates income and taxes to subsidise the other two.

Ideally, the minimum Eco-living-standard must be provided regardless of earning and employment status. But if the budget does not cover the Eco-welfare costs, then it should be means tested, so it is free to those who cannot afford all or part of it and at a reasonable charge for those with enough earnings to cover the costs. In any scenario, the balance must be maintained to sustain the level of the Eco-living-standard for the Eco-city's ecosystem.

The ultimate goal of the administration is to manage the Eco-city's Eco-production departments to generate income for the Eco-welfare front-line services and if there is enough budget, to spend more on the Eco-city's infrastructure without borrowing. The administration's success or failure depends on its ability to maintain the living standard for each Ecolist and maintain the self-sufficiency and sustainability of the Eco-city without borrowing.

PART 3

Selection and Election

The Eco-Criteria of Selection

The Eco-criteria of selection qualifies candidates possessing the abilities and relevant ethical achievements to carry out certain responsibilities in running a service for the Eco-city. The selection includes interviews with the Eco-supreme-judge and the Eco-mayor. After selecting the eligible candidates, the Ecolists vote to choose the right person for the right job.

The candidate not only has to meet the criteria of selection and convince the Eco-supreme-judge and the Eco-mayor but also has to convince people through a manifesto and a programme of improvements to enhance the Ecolists' wellbeing and living standard. Additionally, will resign, subject to prosecution, upon failure, misleading, misconduct and not improving people's wellbeing or fulfilling the promised manifesto.

There are three tiers to govern the Eco-city in a tripartite system: Ecolists, Eco-councillors and Eco-committees.

Note: Initially, interim committees are selected by the Eco-mayor to set the criteria for accepting Ecolists and businesses into the Eco-city. Subsequently, the Ecolists elect the committees after a new selection of candidates has taken place. The process is repeated every five years or in a by-election to replace anyone who fails. There are no political parties in the Eco-city, donors or lobbyists to influence any candidate for any governance position.

Accepting Ecolists

The criteria for selecting suitable Ecolists to live in the Eco-city might vary slightly from one time to another or from one Eco-city to another. The objective is to solve a national, social and humane collection of problems.

In a society where the gap between the poor and rich is vast, a solution must narrow that gap and level the playing field among them. The rich do not need the social welfare to take care of them. On the contrary, the rich are required to invest in people for the mutual benefits of both. The poor, the helpless, the homeless, the elderly, the disabled and the most vulnerable in society need the utmost care from the rich, who will invest and accept a reasonable return on investment as outlined in the Eco-businesses' Eco-socio-economic system.

The most critical condition in the criteria is to create a harmonised Eco-society that can coexist without the negative influences of cultural differences or a language barrier. The integration into one culture is the logical option to avoid conflicts, unify communication means and synergistically increase productivity. Although the Eco-city has various sections and may accommodate diverse cultures, it is better to accommodate only those with minor differences between them. As the saying goes: "Birds of a feather flock together."

For example, Europeans share similar values and cultures, including Russians, North Americans, Australians and other modern democratic countries. Although there are slight differences between them, it would be easier for them to integrate into one culture and adapt to a modern Western Eco-socio-economic system.

Most Muslims, Chinese, Indians, Africans, Middle Easterners and those from other societies in the Far East would find it more challenging to adapt, integrate, accept the Eco-principles and change quickly. Nevertheless, there are exceptions. Some individuals, like me, who originally came from Lebanon, adapt quickly and integrate with Western societies easily.

Unfortunately, the Eco-city is not a social experiment to blend cultures and try to change the Muslims' faith so they become atheists or stop the Indians eating their spices and accept cohabitation without marriage. It is best to create criteria to filter cultures and select those with close similarities to live together and avoid the conflicts of various cultures, which is to ensure the peace and harmony of the Eco-society.

However, up to 5% of selected foreign cultures may integrate with a native one, but a higher percentage becomes harder to control with limited resources and may disturb the peace and harmony of an Eco-society abiding by a specific Eco-socio-economic system and its Eco-principles.

Muslims and other cultures could build their own Eco-cities, create their own Eco-societies and adapt them to their Sharia laws, but they cannot force the Christians (or other religious groups) to follow their Sharia laws. Indians and other cultures could create their own Eco-societies, hoping that, eventually, everybody will integrate into a universal Eco-culture.

To ensure a more harmonious society, the criteria of selection gets filtered down to those with a clean criminal record, i.e. those who have never been in prison or prosecuted for severe offences or misconduct. Moreover, it is filtered down to those who are atheists or do not have extreme religious views. The list goes on to eliminate those who are not suitable for living the Eco-lifestyle in the Eco-city or adapting to its Eco-principles and abiding by them.

The reason for the variable criteria is because they must correspond to the available infrastructure and the demand for particular skills at the time of selection, in addition to resolving a national economic issue for the jobless or reducing the number of social-benefits claimants. In any scenario, the Eco-councillors and business committees make the policy and the psychological profilers select those who fit the required criteria at the time of selection.

Selecting the Eco-councillors

The Eco-councillors selection is defined in the Eco-criteria-for-selection. The best Eco-psychologists, Eco-philosophers and Eco-judges in the Eco-city set the Eco-criteria-for-selection required for each candidate in authority. Then, the voters elect them for their expertise, manifestos and merits, but vote them out when they fail to deliver, commit any misconduct or abuse the trust and authority given to them by the public, without compensation and subject to prosecution.

The primary requirements of the criteria are ethical conduct, a record of accomplishments, appropriate abilities, loyalty, patriotism for the Eco-city, relevant education and specialisation, relevant experience and an achievable vision for improvement or a manifesto/programme for a better standard of living for the Eco-city.

The process of selection and election will have further principles and rules to prevent any financial support being given to the candidates or any external influence. The candidates' information will be open to the public for transparency, including their bank accounts and then the selected candidates will present to the Ecolists the promised manifesto for the electorate to choose the most suitable candidate.

The voters can opt to remove Eco-councillors from power at any time if they fail to deliver their promised declaration.

Electing the Eco-Councillors

The Eco-supreme-judge supervises the election and the appointment of all the Eco-councillors, Eco-committees and any authorities in the Eco-city. The candidates' eligibility must be approved by the Eco-supreme-judge and the Eco-mayor after examining their compatibility with the predetermined criteria of selection.

The first position of leadership as an Eco-councillor is determined by the highest majority, while the deputies and assistants can be appointed from the rest of the candidates who passed the criteria for selection and gained a substantial number of votes. This way the Eco-city will not be split into parties and each candidate can always have a position in running an Eco-city service.

The Eco-election is very democratic and abides by the Eco-freedom principle. Therefore, it is not a partisan election and no one should influence the electorate to vote one way or the other, including the Eco-mayor and the Eco-supreme-judge. There should be no advertising posters, leaflets or mail allowed. However, email campaigns, hustings and conferences are admissible. Each candidate should have his/her own website describing themselves, their track records, achievements, proposed manifesto, forum discussions, etc.

The election of the Eco-councillors happens for only one Eco-councillor at a time to give the electorate time to evaluate each candidate for each service or perhaps there could be one or two elections each month.

PART 1

Eco-Finance-Councillor

Henri Maalouf declares:

Ask not what more can I get, but what else can I give to my Eco-city and country.

Considering the size of the Eco-city, it needs an expert financier with a degree in economics and an excellent record of accomplishment to manage businesses and assets worth more than £200 billion and all the related transactions. He or she can appoint specialist bankers, economists, accountants, business persons, tax inspectors and others as assistants and deputies, secretaries and administration staff. As well as the required qualifications, the person's experience and abilities must meet the Eco-code-of-conduct's principles. Ethics and loyalty come first and the councillor should have no vested interests in any other conflict-of-interest business.

The Eco-councillor will share governance with a committee representing small and large businesses, industries, agriculture and representatives of the public's interests.

The Eco-finance activities and decisions impact all other Eco-councillors. Therefore, approving major decisions and budgeting involves all the others. The unilateral budgets of each Eco-council require unanimous agreement from them all. None of the Eco-councillors is more important than the other. All are equal and are cornerstones in building the Eco-city.

It is imperative that each Eco-finance-councillor candidate proposes a manifesto after passing the criteria for selection to qualify as a candidate for the election.

The proposed guidelines are to help with understanding the Eco-finance principles and some of it applies to all other Eco-councillors. These proposed high-level Eco-socio-economic systems are new Eco ideas to help create new Eco-finance systems that are sustainable and capable of withstanding the test of time and any economic turmoil that might happen, nationally or globally.

The primary responsibilities of this full-time job are to find finances for the Eco-city, industries and businesses of all sizes. The management of the Eco-city's banks, personal funds, wages and mortgages for all the citizens and collecting taxes for the local and central government are also the duties of the Eco-finance-councillor.

The Eco-socio-economic system's rules and regulations should not conflict with the central government systems and the Eco-city should contribute a tax percentage that matches the protection and the support received from the national government.

The Eco-finance-councillor distributes certain portions of the collected taxes to cover the projected and approved budgets for each Eco-council, but releases the funds in real time, after agreeing on the necessity of each expenditure or project. The purchases for the approved projects and spending must go through a transparent bidding process and it must be verified that they are excellent-value-for-money products or services.

The following sections describe some of the key responsibilities of the Eco-finance-councillor and the team of deputies and assistants.

Eco-Monetary-Exchange Mechanisms

Cash is no longer critical for any form of payment and, in time, it will vanish. The Eco-city will support a cashless system in a cashless society. The Ecolists can exchange financial transactions and services among them using a digital Eco-monetary-exchange mechanism. The digital monetary transactions can be encrypted and recorded on special Eco-credit-debit-cards that are synchronised with the Eco-city's website and controlled by the Eco-banks.

The Eco-credit-debit-cards include not only all the financial, transactions and services but also the health and history records of each Ecolist, maintained from the cradle to the grave.

There are four types of Eco-credit-debit-card to use inside and outside the Eco-city: Eco-credit-debit-life (ECDL), Eco-credit-debit-virtual (ECDV), Eco-credit-debit-employment (ECDE) and Eco-credit-debit-commercial (ECDC). An Eco-card-reader is used to update the account balance on the card and synchronise it with the Eco-city's banking website.

ECDL Card

The ECDL card is for everyone and is compulsory to record the cost of living from birth to death. It also combines the transactions on all the other cards, including taxes, debts, income and equities inside and outside the Eco-city.

The Eco-welfare costs, such as health, education and other free services, must be recorded on the ECDL card to account for the cost of living of any unproductive times from birth till death. The rationale behind it is to calculate the cost of the Eco-welfare system, raise taxes to match it and maintain the sustainability of the Eco-city's ecosystem.

Note: In *Ecolism 2*, under the research and innovations section, there is information about a micro SD card capable of holding 2TB of data, which is large enough to store a lifetime's records about each individual. These records on the SD card can be synchronised with the personal profile of each person.

ECDV Card

The ECDV card is a cashless card specially designed for the Ecolists' to exchange goods and services among them without paying or receiving any cash in any currency inside the Eco-city.

For example, if I owe someone X amount of credit and others owe me Y amount, this is used to establish my account's balance. But there is a limit to how much I can owe the others. Initially, everyone must work to build the Eco-city or do something for the Eco-city's administration and receives virtual credit that can be used to exchange credit with others.

The reason for this concept is to exchange services or goods that a person can offer to others and receive an equivalent in return.

ECDE Card

The ECDE card is mainly for monetary transactions when working in the Eco-city and its surrounding industries, as an employee receiving an hourly rate or monthly salary. It includes information about income, taxes, purchases, debts, mortgage repayments and any other monetary transactions for revenue and expenditure.

This ECDE card is necessary to efficiently work out the taxes paid and equalise it with the cost of the Eco-welfare system.

ECDC Card

The ECDC card is mainly for money exchange outside the Eco-city for the self-employed and businesses. The ECDC can be locally issued by the Eco-city's commercial bank. However, an Eco-resident must register in the Eco-city all their accounts, cards and any business interests outside the Eco-city.

The rationale behind the local registration of any national or global business interests is for transparency and accountability. The taxes on income earned externally or internally while operating from the Eco-city, including internet transactions, must be paid locally, abiding by local rules. And the losses of a parent company outside the Eco-city must not impact local profits or be offset against them.

Eco-Card Clarification

This clarification is to avoid any confusion and to justify the rationale for using different types of cards.

The ECDL arguably replaces all other cards, but it is added on, as a backup and collective information about all other Eco-cards. Such an important card must be kept in a safe place or never leave the Eco-home and is always synchronised with the

Eco-city's website. It is not something every person should carry around and risk compromising personal records.

The ECDV is not an actual cash-transaction card. It is an 'I owe you' debit-credit card, with no interest until paid for or credit is exchanged with another service.

The ECDE is the daily card used as a standard debit-credit card, but it has extra information about the global balance of each person, including the mortgage balance and other equities.

The ECDC is for use outside the Eco-city and is isolated from the exchanges inside the Eco-city.

Eco-City-Bank

The Eco-city-bank is not a business or trading organisation, but it is a controlled and transparent accountancy firm that records and protects all financial transactions. The Eco-city-bank directly reports to the Eco-city's Eco-finance-councillor and not shareholders. It complies with the local Eco-principles and all the operations go through the Eco-Citibank's website.

It is also similar to a high-street bank that does not trade with any risky business or investments to maintain its long-term sustainability and avoid any possible bankruptcy.

The principal function of the Eco-city-bank is to manage the Eco-city's mortgages and earnings for those locally employed in local industries, businesses, agriculture and local authorities. Conjointly, it collaborates with the Eco-city-commercial-bank to ensure that the income of the self-employed will be transferred to the Eco-city-bank to pay the taxes, outstanding mortgages and other debts.

The Eco-city-bank is strictly local and does not engage in any commercial trading activity outside the Eco-city. It is purposely set up to manage the Eco-city's financial affairs, including the Eco-administration and the residents, trading with each other.

The Eco-city-bank issues and monitors the ECDL, ECDV and ECDE cards. The ECDL card will help the Eco-welfare system and Eco-finance councillor to plan and adjust the tax revenue to cover the cost of living for the required lifestyle. It is crucial to record the expenditure on Eco-welfare from birth and during unproductive years to plan the tax-revenue level required to cover the costs and maintain the sustainability of the Eco-socio-economic system.

After accepting Ecolists to live in the Eco-city, it will be standard practice to grant them a credit loan of £100,000 to cover the mortgage loan on an Eco-home, provided that they have no other source of finance or equity.

The Eco-welfare system pays the monthly interest on the credit loan until the Eco-council finds a job for the unemployed, then changes it to repayment after employment has commenced and deducts it at the source of income, which is paid into the ECDE account.

The Eco-city-bank also issues the ECDV card to help the poor and unemployed to live in a cashless society through locally exchanging services or goods. This card is for people without any cash to spend, who can find no work to do, but need or can offer a service locally.

For example, a plumber can do a job for an electrician and charge per hour using ECDV; the plumber can then use this virtual credit to pay an electrician to do electrical work for him or her and so on. This way, the Ecolists exchange services between them. It is not only services but also trading with food or just borrowing from each other without a guarantee of being paid back, to improve the trust between the Ecolists and adapt to the charitable behaviour of helping each other.

All the Eco-city card accounts can be viewed and accessed on the local website of the Eco-city-bank for the Ecolists to manage the transactions between them and immediately check on their daily account balances.

Eco-City-Commercial-Bank

The Eco-city-commercial-bank is the only bank allowed to handle all the buying and selling inside and outside the Eco-city for all the industries, businesses, agriculture, IT and the self-employed.

The taxes are deducted at source to ensure there is no tax evasion or debt avoidance. The separation between the Eco-city-bank and the Eco-city-commercial-bank is necessary to ensure the sustainable endurance and self-sufficiency of the Eco-city.

If all the industries fail and the Eco-city is isolated from the rest of the world, then people can still survive.

Any global business must be licensed to operate in the Eco-city, given an Eco-name to become entirely independent of any parent company and abide by the Eco-city rules and principles.

The Eco-city-commercial-bank will facilitate business loans and deduct taxes at source on all Eco-sales, using a balanced taxation formula, to maintain the sustainability of the Eco-city and encourage investors.

All industrial and business transactions must pass through the Eco-city-commercial-bank to allow the Eco-tax-inspectors to monitor the accounts, assess the taxes that should be paid and collect them at their source. The Eco-tax-inspectors will have full access to the bank's accounts and ensure that all transactions are transparent and justified.

The Eco-city-commercial-bank also issues the ECDC card

for the self-employed and businesses to help each person or organisation monitor their daily transactions and the balances of their accounts.

Business-Eco-Tax System

As Jesus said: "Give back to Caesar the things of Caesar and to God the things of God."

The Eco-tax is a fairer and balanced proportional tax that progresses with an increase in profits or turnover according to the Eco-taxation rules of the Eco-city. However, to protect any investment from losses due to excessive taxation, a tax-free 5% is accounted for as the cost of investment and not profits and the progressive tax formula is after the 5% tax-free margin.

As an example, the investor may keep the investment in a bank and earn 1% interest or borrow from a bank at 2% interest. So, to encourage investment in the business, agriculture or industry, we must give the investor an incentive of a guaranteed percentage that is higher than the borrowing rate from a bank.

The example assumes borrowing at 2% interest and, as an incentive to invest, the tax system allows 3% guaranteed profit to make it up to 5% tax-free net profit. The bank can borrow from the government at 0.5% interest and should be happy to lend at 1% to 2% interest. With this formula, everyone is happy. The bank is making money; the investor has guaranteed profits on investment. Consequently, jobs can be created and the Eco-city can collect taxes to spend on the wellbeing of the Ecolists and the excess on its infrastructure.

Progressive tax charged must have criteria and simple rules to limit the allowed exemptions for expenditure from the gross turnover; for example, the agreed cost of raw materials, workers' wages, other approved operating costs and reinvesting in local in local research. In a nutshell, these are approved and limited overhead costs disassociated from a parent company's losses or spending outside the Eco-city.

The investor should obtain an Eco-licence to operate from the Eco-city as an independent local business. The global parent company for the same firm can assist in sales and provide knowledge to receive the profits after tax, but it cannot offset expenditure or losses abroad against local ones.

The Eco-city's taxation system is more efficient, less bureaucratic and fairer than others. Calculating and collecting taxes at source is much more efficient in the Eco-city than by the national government, because all the transactions pass through the Eco-city-commercial-bank, which is under the control of the Eco-finance-councillor and is transparent to the Eco-tax-inspectors.

The level of monthly earnings that cover living costs, such as mortgage interest, food and other vital expenses is always ring-fenced from paying taxes. It is similar to the threshold set for the minimum allowance of a tax-free income. Note: Where income is less than the cost of living, then the Eco-welfare system will subsidise to equalise. But if it is more than the minimum living cost, then contributions and taxes shall be deducted at source or paid directly by the employer.

The tax formulas and the rates can be adjusted to balance the Eco-city's Eco-welfare costs, infrastructure requirements and paying a portion to the central government. The challenge is to modify the taxation percentage to attract investment, enable global competition and cover the costs of a decent living standard.

Eco-Welfare Costs

The big question is, how do we calculate the Eco-welfare cost?

On average, if people live for up to 84 years and work for 42 years, then the tax they pay during their productive years should cover their living costs for the 42 unproductive years. To elaborate further and as a general rule for easy reference, a child needs Eco-welfare and education till the age of 25; that is, until they get a degree, train in new skills and have time to find a job.

Then, with any luck, they will work for 42 productive years and retire at 67. After retiring, they will need additional Eco-welfare support between the ages of 67 and 84. So, 17 plus 25 years accumulates to 42 unproductive years.

Logically, the 42 productive years should pay enough taxes for the 84-year lifespan; otherwise, upsetting the balance of this formula will upset the balance of the Eco-city's ecosystem and this leads to an unsustainable economy.

Note: The assumption of age or productive years varies from one person to another, depending on abilities and lifespan, but the balance remains the same and the excess somewhere may compensate for shortfalls somewhere else.

Eco-Income and Hourly Rate

Now, let us put figures into an example and assume the cost of living is £500/month, including mortgage interest. This means each person must earn £1,000/month minimum and pay £500/month in taxes to live for 84 years with guaranteed decent Eco-welfare and front-line services. Naturally, people can work more, earn more, spend more, live better and afford more luxuries or holidays.

So, what should be the minimum hourly rate in an Eco-city to provide the necessities of survival for a person living 84 years? Well, there are few variables of the equation to consider.

We are not all physically and mentally equal, nor can we continuously work for eight hours a day until we retire. When we are younger, we can work over 12 hours/day and gradually decrease to ten, then eight hours and so on. At 65, people might be able to work efficiently for five hours until they have age-related ailments and lesser abilities.

Therefore, the best solution is to make the working hours' system more flexible than the existing global one and reduce it to five-hour shifts with the provision that people can work two shifts or more if capable. This way, the increase and decrease of daily working hours throughout a lifetime will balance the most productive days with the less productive ones.

So, assuming we work ten hours a day and five days a week for 22 days a month, this means we work 220 hours a month. Considering the cost of living in the Eco-city, including interest on the mortgage that is £500/month only, then we should be able to accept £1,000/220hrs = ~£4.50 an hour, out of which £2.25 is the Eco-tax contribution to pay for the Eco-welfare that costs £500/month throughout the 42 non-productive years.

It's worth noting that the tax can be reduced if there is enough revenue from the industries and businesses. Otherwise, the employer pays the tax for the employee. People can work more years, more days a week or more hours a day to have more money in the pot for more Eco-welfare allowances in their retirement or put money aside for rainy days or unforeseen events.

Note: The £500/month cost of living considers £250/month interest on the mortgage and living an Eco-lifestyle in the Eco-city. However, if a couple is working and living in the same Eco-home, then they can afford a £500/month repayment.

In the Eco-city, there is no electric bill to pay and no insurances, TV licence, water bill, transport costs, bank charges, lawyer's fees, luxury clothes, entertainment costs or any other outgoings. The food is also cheap, can be grown in the Eco-city in each garden of the Eco-home and most of it could be free.

Employment Eco-Tax

The same Eco-tax contribution principle for the workers applies to the self-employed or small businesses. They must pay the compulsory minimum Eco-tax contribution and a tax rate on profits. The industries and businesses will pay the employees' taxes directly to the Eco-finance department via the Eco-city-bank.

The Eco-city will spend the taxes on the Eco-welfare system, front-line services and its infrastructure improvements to raise the Eco-living-standards for the improved wellbeing of the Ecolists.

The Eco-taxation system charges lower taxes for businesses to help them become more profitable and more competitive and to encourage them to move to the Eco-city. But, at the same time, balances the revenue with the expenditure to avoid borrowings and budget deficit.

Eco-Tax-Inspectors

The Eco-finance-councillor will appoint Eco-tax-inspectors at each medium and large business, with full and transparent access to monitor any sales or expenditures to ensure that the industry pays the right taxes after the allowed overheads and minimum 5% tax-free profits.

The Eco-tax-inspectors will rotate between companies to inspect their accounts and inspect each other's work too. If any is corrupt, they will be severely penalised, losing all assets locally and globally. Additionally, they will be named and shamed, sent on a rehabilitation programme and retrained in a different type of job.

The Eco-industries and Eco-businesses must use an account in the Eco-city-commercial-bank for all their sales and expenditure, complying with the terms and conditions of operating in the Eco-city. It is to ensure complete transparency and the collecting of taxes at source. However, the net profits can be transferred to any global bank or parent company after paying the local taxes.

It is imperative for sustainability that local sales are taxed locally and overheads are agreed locally. Any operating business or industry must have a local Eco-name and an Eco-licence to function independently from any parent company and must abide by the Eco-city's rules.

PART 2

Eco-Industry-Councillor

Henri Maalouf declares:

If profits are made from the locals, then taxes must be paid to benefit the locals.

The locals must buy locally produced products to keep themselves employed and remain self-sufficient in a sustainable ecosystem.

The Eco-industry-councillor, like every other Eco-councillor, must pass the Eco-criteria-for-selection first, then be elected and operate in an analogous way to the Eco-finance-councillor, using similar systems and relevant departments, but more suitable for industry.

The Eco-industry-councillor must be a subject-matter expert in an industry or hold a degree in electro-mechanics or an equivalent. Also, he/she must have a successful record of accomplishments in managing industries worth around £100 billion and a knowledge of global markets. Eco-councillors should share power with the representatives' committees for the industries and workforce.

These guidelines are to help with understanding the Eco-industries' principles and concepts.

Ecolists should try to buy and use locally manufactured goods and export the excess to keep the import/export balance right. The Eco-industry-councillor will ensure that the Eco-industries of the Eco-city will produce what it needs at a specially agreed price and sell the excess outside the Eco-city at competitive market prices.

The available products in the Eco-city will be limited varieties of approved Eco-products that are compatible with the Eco-city's standards and requirements. For example, the same type of ovens, coolers, houses, furniture, etc. This uniformity is essential for a classless society, equality among the Ecolists and to maintain the same level and value when somebody moves from one Eco-home to another.

The principal terms and conditions for industries to operate in the Eco-city are to comply with keeping CO_2 and N_2O emissions and other environmental pollutants' levels to zero. Also, they must train and employ local Ecolists and use the Eco-city-commercial-bank for all their sales, expenditure and purchases. The Eco-council and Ecolists will retain the voting power to remove any industry's CEO from office, upon any misconduct, failure to make the industry profitable or maintain the Ecolists' employment.

It is vital to watch CEOs' activities to prevent them running the industry down to sell it cheaper to different shareholders or allow an aggressive takeover. It is also essential to monitor employees and especially engineers, to prevent any industrial espionage or sabotage.

The Eco-city, on the other hand, will give the industries free electricity; cheap leasehold land; protection; competitive hourly rates for good-quality, vetted employees; IT facilities; a 5% tax-free margin on investment; and other services to ensure their global competitiveness.

The Eco-city will not allow unions that may instigate industrial action and cause business disruption. The workers earn hourly rates; the more they work, the more they make.

This Eco-employment system is necessary to maintain harmony, security, guaranteed profitability and competitiveness, which encourages investors to invest and employ locals.

However, whistle-blowing and petitions can be brought to the committees and the Eco-councillors to take action against unfairness, misconduct and the wrongdoings of the businesses' management.

The centralised IT data and call centres will offer the industries efficient and competitively priced services for their sales, software applications and their IT infrastructure.

The Eco-city will also provide the industries with security and services 24/7, including quality Eco-workers who are skilled and trained in the job at competitive hourly rates and a low-rate taxation system. The flexibility of the locals working on hourly rates is necessary to enable industries to expand or shrink quickly to maintain their sustainability in an industrial ecosystem.

The Eco-industries will not necessarily manufacture either the cheapest products or the most expensive products. Instead, they will manufacture the best value for money that lasts longer. The Eco-quality products will be built to last and guaranteed for 25 years to become the most economical merchandise in the long term.

As an illustration, consider the following. If we manufacture a high-quality car that costs £20,000 and would last 20 years with minimum maintenance, which requires £100/year only, it will be cheaper than a car that costs £10,000 but needs £1,000 a year in maintenance costs and lasts eight years.

The Eco-industries have the potential to employ all the

unemployed Eco-workers for as many hours as they can work, both physically and mentally and, hopefully, will bring back the old industrial revolution in a new form as the Eco-industrial-revolution.

The Eco-city has the potential to become equivalent to a commercial capital city such as London, generating billions of pounds sterling and paying taxes to increase the value of the gross domestic product (GDP) or the market value of goods and services, to help the country's budget deficit.

The struggling local and global industries in the country can downsize, restructure and move to the Eco-city to benefit from lower overheads, a cheaper skilled workforce, an innovations centre and the immediate market demand to build the first one million Eco-homes for the Eco-city with all the required furniture.

Some industries might take advantage of the Eco-city's three million consumers to start up their core operations, expand and sell Eco-products outside the Eco-city, while others could benefit from low overheads and become globally competitive.

The Eco-city must be self-sufficient and locally manufacture most of what is needed to build it. The challenge is to accept moving to the Eco-city those who can work in the available jobs of the Eco-industries that will start building the Eco-city and manufacture the products it needs. The same rule applies to the workforce required for agricultural businesses and other services.

When the infrastructure becomes ready, then other people can move in as soon as there are available front-line services to accommodate them. This will be the first mission of the Eco-council: to organise its logistics.

Eco-Research-and-Innovations

Henri Maalouf declares:

Why waste the talents, when they can make you rich?

The Eco-industry-councillor can appoint a deputy to run research and innovations. The Eco-research-and-innovation-centre will be open for all scientists, university graduates, engineers and innovators from around the world to create new Eco-industries. The Eco-research-and-innovation-centre will also organise exhibitions for international investors to promote Eco-related ideas and inventions. The Eco-city's industries and business experts will help to validate the designs, support the innovators and manufacture the products to turn dreams into reality.

The Eco-finance-councillor will help with sourcing investment for the tested innovative ideas, while the Eco-justice-councillor will protect the copyright for the inventor or research groups. The Eco-research-and-innovation-centre will give opportunities to any talented specialists to enhance the Eco-city's manufacturing industry and to sell their products to generate revenue.

PART 3

Eco-Business-Councillor

Henri Maalouf declares:

When the balance of mutual interests is maintained, long-term success can be sustained.

The Eco-business-councillor, like every other Eco-councillor, must pass the Eco-criteria-for-selection first, then be elected and operate in a comparable manner to the Eco-finance-councillor, using similar systems and relevant departments, but more suitable for the business service.

The Eco-business-councillor must be a subject-matter expert in small and large business, hold a relevant business or management university degree, have a successful-enough track record to manage £100-billion-worth of commercial activities and understand markets and business services, especially selling, buying, importing and exporting.

These guidelines are to help with understanding the Eco-business principles and concepts.

Eco-businesses and Eco-services may do the same business as the City of London or New York, comprising small businesses, call centres, sales companies, insurance companies, the stock exchange, investment companies, wealth-management companies and others.

However, most of the business activities are outside the Eco-city and the Eco-businesses must remain ethical to gain an excellent global reputation.

The Eco-business-councillor will not accept rogue traders who lie and make money at any expense, even harming others.

In the 21st century, some merchants or business people have the immorality to sabotage or bankrupt a company, a bank or the country for the sake of making profits at any cost. Such practices are forbidden in the Eco-city and the business-security teams monitor, investigate and scrutinise each activity.

The business model in the 21st century is profiteering at any cost and money before ethics and globalisation, without national protection or interests. Business globalisation does not belong to any country. It belongs to a virtual state that does not physically exist and travels across borders duty-free or tax-free. Therefore, global businesses avoid paying national taxes to countries they make their profits from and their virtual state becomes their tax haven.

The Eco-business employers put employees' protection first, ethics and good value for money second, then guaranteed reasonable profits and paying a fair share of taxes to keep the business running and sustainable in the long term.

The Eco-business section in the sustenance area of the Eco-city will attract big businesses to build their luxurious Eco-buildings and have global business centres. They will benefit from vetted employees available 24/7 and flexible working hours at very competitive rates. Electricity is free and they can install their own renewable sources of energy. Furthermore, a tax-free margin can be agreed for various types of businesses, depending on their turnover.

The IT data centre will provide computer-system facilities to help the businesses to locally and globally perform their operations. The Eco-industries will need immense sales power to promote and sell their products outside the Eco-city. Therefore, the Eco-call-centres will provide sales and support services to promote the Eco-products globally.

The Eco-businesses must operate in the most economical way, but maintain a high-quality standard, give good value for money and compete with the rest of the world. The high efficiency and productivity combined with lower overheads are the main Eco-business principles for competitiveness.

Some reasons for the Indians' ability to offer offshore services at low prices are because they work hard and are not limited by working hours' laws. They work as cooperative teams and run services for several businesses simultaneously from the same place so that there is no time wasted and they accept lower income because their cost of living is much less.

The Germans have rules like the rest of Europe, the USA and other countries, which includes working less than 40 hours a week. However, I have seen Germans working from 7am to 7pm without asking for extra money. The Koreans work ten hours a day as a standard and work hard as one team.

So, if we combine the practices of all the successful business models of others and do even better, then we can improve productivity and become the ideal Eco-business.

The Eco-businesses in the Eco-city are not necessarily centralised in one commercial centre or monopolised by large enterprises only. Instead, they are in multiple locations and virtual offices. They spread across the Eco-city and each Eco-home in a controlled way. Each Ecolist may work as many hours as he or she likes from home. The older work fewer hours, while the younger work more. The fees paid are for productive working hours and achieved tasks, while idle time is not chargeable.

However, sometimes commitments to some hours or shift work are the requirement of a job. The business model of a monthly salary allows people to earn a total wage whether they have worked 40 hours a week or less and whether they were productive or not or idle half the time. It is unfair for businesses to pay for the idle time, but it is also their responsibility to keep the workers busy and make the best out of their time.

The Ecolists in the Eco-city can adapt to this flexible, Eco-working hourly rate system because they live a more economical Eco-lifestyle and the Eco-welfare system compensates for the idle hours. The Eco-working model is simple, logical and fair for investors and workers. The investor gets a good return on investment and becomes very competitive, the worker earns more from their achievements and the consumer benefits from excellent-value-for-money prices.

The advantages of the Eco-business model allow the company to be much more competitive because of the lower overheads, 24/7 availability to match global working hours and the Eco-ethics of running a business, which build its worldwide reputation.

There are no pensions for a company to worry about, no strikes that affect its operation and no pay for idle time or unproductivity. The Eco-city's welfare system will take care of people's pensions in a free Eco-home with all the required facilities, food and front-line services and compensate for the idle time where no work is available.

In the Eco-business-centre, some employees work as one force in a pool for one or more companies, so they are busy at all times and the workload is distributed between them. The group of employees works in an open space and quickly exchange information between them for better service, passing knowledge for quick training on the job and continuous improvements.

The Eco-socio-economic system succeeds and becomes globally competitive if everyone in the Eco-city joins hands and works as one conglomerate company with many departments, businesses, industries, agriculture, workforce and investments all in one and under the same banner.

When the Eco-city works as one conglomerate, a factory does not need a sales force and will contract the Eco-businesses to take care of their sales. Also, it does not require IT professionals and lets the Eco-ICT-data-centre provide that service. It does not need to invest in research and allows the Eco-research-and-innovation-centre to do that work for them.

Loan sharks also may not operate in the Eco-city and no lender will charge interest of over 5% above the Bank of England's base rate, even if they use their money from outside the Eco-city-bank. Therefore, one of the Eco-business-councillor's responsibilities is to license only ethical businesses and blacklist all those with immoral history, including gambling games in any form or shape.

The Eco-city is not interested in making money by any means necessary. Otherwise, businesses in the Eco-city would not be called an Eco-business, which means it is ethical, has fair terms and conditions, makes reasonable profits and does not take advantage of the weakness of others to bankrupt them and make them pay severe penalties.

The Eco-businesses can build their luxury buildings, employ vetted locals and hire experts from outside the Eco-city, provided that they are ethical.

The Eco-businesses have the advantage of selling all the Eco-city's industrial and agricultural products and all types of services. The Eco-city can offer hundreds of thousands of self-employed people working from home, especially for call centres, at an incredibly competitive hourly rate, where they are paid as they productively work and there is no payment for idle time.

The flexibility of the Eco-working system is also suitable for the retired, the physically challenged, parents raising children and the unemployed, who may become partially employed until they find a better job.

The Eco-sales-power and pools of sales personnel will also have enormous purchasing power and may convince manufacturers to move to the Eco-city to supply it with cheaper products because of the lower overheads and free facilities and sell outside the Eco-city.

PART 4

Eco-Welfare-Councillor

Henri Maalouf declares:

My Eco-home is my space for survival and the Eco-city is my paradise.

The Eco-welfare-councillor, like every other Eco-councillor, must pass the Eco-criteria-for-selection first, then be elected and operate in an equivalent manner to the Eco-finance-councillor and others, using similar systems and relevant departments, but more suitable for the Eco-housing and Eco-welfare services.

The Eco-welfare-councillor must be a subject-matter expert in city planning and wellbeing issues; should preferably have a degree in law, management or an equivalent; and must have an unbeaten track record to manage the accommodation for one million homes. Therefore, they must have strong abilities for organising, planning and other qualities.

These guidelines are to help with understanding the Eco-housing and Eco-welfare principles and concepts.

Eco-Housing

The demand for housing in the UK, the USA and the rest of the world is accelerating at a higher rate than building them. Even if we create one million new houses in a country or state to cover the demand, by the time we finish the construction, there will be new requirements for another million or more.

Therefore, building new Eco-cities should become the norm and the trend. With high foresight, if we must build, let's do it right and build Eco-homes organised in an Eco-city and accompanied by a fairer, new Eco-socio-economic system, because it is better to make a new car than to keep trying to repair an old one.

The proposed Eco-solution of this new Eco-concept is to provide an Eco-home with straightforward terms of ownership, but enforce repossession upon non-compliance with the Eco-city's principles and its Eco-socio-economic ecosystem.

The minimum Eco-living-standard is that each couple of Ecolists occupy a three-bedroomed Eco-home and have two children. The Eco-socio-economic system entitles every couple older than 16 to own an Eco-home with free facilities such as electricity, water, an Eco-personal-computer (Eco-PC) with internet access, free transport and an edible garden to grow food and become self-sufficient.

These facilities allow any individual to study and work from home, accessing the world via the internet, survive from an edible garden and exchange services or food with others using the ECDV card in a cashless society that can withstand any global or national economic depression, isolation or even wars.

The benefits of the Eco-concept are to provide Eco-homes in a new Eco-socio-economic system, converting the unemployed and unproductive to becoming employed, saving on government social benefits and giving the poorest of the society a dignified life and a secure future.

The Eco-home has an Eco-socio-economic purpose and function and is not just a shelter to rest. In the old days, an Englishman's home was his castle. Nowadays, in our competitive world, we have to race for our survival and cope with the ever-demanding socio-economic systems. Therefore, a house should serve an additional purpose, become a functional space for living and have facilities to learn new skills and work remotely to produce supplementary income.

The Eco-homes are identical across most of the Eco-city; hence, moving from one house to another is possible and flexible. The Eco-principles encourage stability and sustainability, but if a couple needs to split, then it is possible to find another partner or friend and exchange places. It is one of the Eco-housing-councillor's responsibilities to make the transition smooth.

However, each person owns a share in a house or an investment and, since all the Eco-homes are identical, the person's equity moves to the new Eco-home and will have the same value. Eventually, people reach retirement age and move to the perimeter of the Eco-city, where more suitable accommodation is designed for them and they take their equity with them. When people eventually die, they can pass their assets to their children tax-free or give it back to the Eco-city to help others.

The Eco-housing-councillor has a challenging task to organise people's accommodation and track where everybody lives. It is also difficult to match couples living under the same roof, whether as friends or as loving couples. But it is an Eco-covenant for people to share for economic and social reasons. People should live an Eco-lifestyle and learn how to compromise in similar ways to Scandinavians residing in harmonised societies as groups of non-biological families.

Eco-Welfare

Henri Maalouf declares:

A contented society is more productive than a depressed one.

Eco-welfare is vital for the Ecolists to ensure their wellbeing, happiness, harmony, peaceful living and maximum productivity. The Eco-welfare system has Eco-carers who work with Eco-psychologists and Eco-security to help the Ecolists with their problems or disputes.

The Eco-carers try to resolve issues amicably or ask the psychiatrists for the right course of action and appropriate rehabilitation treatment if necessary. If there is an act of violence, the Eco-security intervenes and escalates it to the Eco-justice or a rehabilitation centre if needed.

If all fails and the same offences are repeated, as a last resort, people can be expelled from the Eco-city, losing all their equity. This action is necessary as a deterrent to stop people from reoffending.

The Eco-welfare system is responsible for the wellbeing of the Ecolists from birth till the final days of life and works with all Eco-councillors to ensure the quality of life for all.

The Ecolists cannot afford to pay for insurance. Therefore, if an accident happens or a disaster, the Eco-city will deal with any arising issues or incidents.

The Eco-carers are multilevel teams of various specialisations and must be trained to deal with numerous types of issues and consult specialists to address particular kinds of problem.

Each Eco-carer group has a responsibility to address a particular social issue. The Eco-healthcare ensures that everyone is fit to work physically and mentally. A group of carers for education and skills training ensure that the unemployed have the right skills for the required jobs in the Eco-city. A group of financial advisors help people with budgeting, living within their means, guide the self-employed in how to run a successful business and so on.

PART 5

Eco-Energy-and-Water-Councillor

Henri Maalouf declares:

If we protect our environment, nature will protect us.

The Eco-energy-and-water-councillor, like every other Eco-councillor, must pass the Eco-criteria-for-selection first, then stand for election and operate in a similar manner to the others, using similar systems and relevant departments, but more suitable for the Eco-energy and Eco-water services.

The Eco-energy-and-water-councillor must be a subject-matter expert in Eco-energy, hold a master's or PhD degree in electrical engineering or equivalent and must have an efficacious track record to manage the energy and water requirements of a large Eco-city.

These guidelines are to help to understand the Eco-energy principles and concept.

The concept is to ensure that the Eco-city and its industries are self-sufficient in producing sufficient energy to meet their needs from renewable sources, including the collection of water from rainfall and other sources.

The ultimate achievement of the Eco-energy systems is to

work with the industries and the Eco-research-and-innovation centre to create more-efficient renewable-energy plants that compete with nuclear, fossil fuels and other forms of energy. After adding substantial enhancements to the renewable-energy systems, the Eco-city can have its own brand of Eco-renewable-energy systems designed to be four times more efficient than the traditional ones.

The current solar panels and wind turbines are 15% efficient, but there are already technological advances to quadruple their efficiency and make a return on investment in four years instead of 16. The advances in science are already making renewable energy more competitive than fossil fuels and nuclear, as illustrated in *Ecolism 2*.

Supplying the Eco-city will revolutionise the renewable-energy industries and, once mass production is in place, exporting to the rest of the world will become more competitive. Then the profits from trading will pay the cost of the investment.

Eco-Water

Henri Maalouf declares:

A planet with water is a planet of life and healthier water is needed for healthier living.

The Eco-water's hygiene and quality are of paramount importance in the Eco-city. The Eco-energy-and-water-councillor ensures that drinking water has the necessary minerals for healthier Ecolists and it is free from harmful particles. Moreover, the water supplies and reserves for irrigation of agriculture must be adequate to survive a climatic drought.

The design of the Eco-city primarily relies on natural rainfall and water stored in the Eco-rivers. Each Eco-home collects rainwater for local consumption and the Eco-rivers store the Eco-city's water for the water plant to process and distribute as required.

PART 6

Eco-Agriculture-Councillor

Henri Maalouf declares:

Give them food for the day, they eat it and ask for more, but give them land to farm, they eat forever and ask no more.

The Eco-agriculture-councillor, like every other Eco-councillor, must pass the Eco-criteria-of-selection first, then stand for election and operate in a comparable manner to the others, using similar systems and relevant departments, but more suitable for the Eco-agriculture service.

The Eco-agriculture-councillor must be a subject-matter expert in agriculture, hold a degree in agriculture so they understand farming and must have a successful-enough record of accomplishment to manage the agricultural requirements of a substantially sized Eco-city.

The following guidelines are to help with understanding the Eco-agriculture principles and concepts.

The primary objective of the Eco-agriculture system is to ensure self-sufficiency and sell the excess of its produce to pay the cost of its overheads and investments.

It is an opportunity to create an Eco-food brand that is

organic, fresh, free from genetic modification and pesticides, good value for money and helps the local farmers.

The Eco-agriculture-councillor's manifesto will lay out plans, projects and policies to achieve this objective.

We must eat what we produce to live self-sufficiently and secure our daily food from our lands, as a national security concern.

A country reliant on importing food to survive is subject to the threat of starvation by the exporters. It is like Greece's dependency on the euro, where Germany can stop supplying them with it to starve their people to death, make them surrender or sign any imposed terms of unfair agreements.

It is imperative in an ideal Eco-socio-economic system to be self-sufficient and to eat what is locally produced instead of relying on someone else that may take advantage of national needs, then blackmail the nation, like banks and financial institutions sometimes do.

However, more competitive agriculture requires cheaper labour, more-efficient machinery and the multi-seasonal utilisation of the same land. Hence, it needs long-term investment instead of small subsidies and the best way to achieve that is to have adequate food for the Eco-city and export enough to pay back the investment.

The big question is, what would we farm? The answer depends on the available resources and health requirements.

First, people should adapt their diet to what we can grow in a particular season and area.

Second, it should be determined what is more profitable to cultivate using an available investment.

Third, we must use the best technology that yields a better return on investment.

Fourth, we must grow food that is more nutritious and costs less.

The large-scale agricultural projects must be feasible, substantial value for money, free from the genetic modification and harmful pesticides.

The Eco-city's stores will collect all the produce from the Eco-city and the agriculture farms. The Eco-stores will hold the crops from the Eco-homes' edible gardens; the streets' berry bushes and trees; the fish from the Eco-rivers; the meat, milk and eggs from the livestock herd and poultry flocks roaming around the Eco-rivers.

The Eco-stores process the Eco-produce to sell to the Ecolists and Eco-restaurants at cost price, but export the rest at market prices as an Eco-organic-brand that is free from chemicals, genetic modification and harmful pesticides.

One of the Eco-health principles is prevention rather than cure to save on higher costs for medical treatment. And, most of the time, the healthiest option is the cheapest. Most Westerners do not eat animal liver, while it is less expensive than meat and much healthier! Chicken eggs have the highest quality protein and nature has provided us with the chicken to deliver them almost free, similarly to cows producing milk.

So why would we buy Indian or Chinese takeaway dinners, Turkish chicken shish, Mexican tacos or other readymade meals that are more expensive than purchasing a whole spit-roast chicken or eating healthier food that is more nutritious and contains more quantities of fresh, local meat from known sources and ingredients?

Why do we need spices from unknown sources or hygiene, if we can grow our own herbs, tomatoes, chillies and spices, subject to our strict Eco-organic controls and Eco-hygiene? The local produce will always be healthier, fresher, of known origin, free from hidden ingredients or dirt and, above all, help to keep the locals employed.

Although Ecolists have edible gardens to grow their vegetables and are able to eat eggs from their chickens, they may not have time for gardening. In this case, they can ask the Eco-stores or others to help and share profits from the produce of their gardens.

The alternative to gardening is to buy from the Eco-stores and cook it or, for more convenience, eat at the Eco-restaurants at cost price to keep their outgoings to a minimum. Note: The Eco-restaurants in the Eco-city are non-profit-making businesses and are run by the Eco-city's agriculture administration to enable the penniless or retired to eat without paying and eliminate the possibility of any hunger as part of fundamental human rights.

If all the above is not enough and the Eco-city residents cannot adapt to what is locally available, then the Eco-city is not suitable for them and they must find somewhere else to live outside the Eco-city. In the Eco-city, the expectations are that people can follow and abide by the Eco-lifestyle and Eco-eating principles.

Henri Maalouf declares:

Eat to survive, not for pleasure; eat what is healthier, not what tastes better.

The Eco-nutritionists would also recommend which herbal medicine to use for curing minor ailments or as a preventative measure. They would create health-education programmes as part of the school curriculum, supported by TV cookery programmes for nutritious and healthier cooking, not based on how the meal looks or tastes. Steaming food is the healthiest method of cooking and people should adapt to it. Baking is healthier than frying with harmful oils that convert to trans-fatty acids and cause bad low-density lipoprotein (LDL) cholesterol that blocks the arteries.

People should listen to the correct advice to prevent heart attacks and expensive medical treatment. The farmers should not produce crops for oils that do not stand high frying temperatures in the first place. Also, the Eco-city should not import such oils and no one should buy them. This is how we apply Eco-nutrition principles:

Henri Maalouf declares:

Prevention rather than cure and if what harms you does not exist, then no harm will come to you.

The Eco-restaurants are available at strategic locations in the Eco-city and at each school, industry or business centre, so people do not waste time in looking for nutritional food or cooking. The Eco-food is locally produced, harvested and consumed while it is still fresh, for the people to benefit from its optimal nutritional value. The Eco-city will not import packaged food that loses some of its nutritional value before it reaches its destination and consumption.

The Eco-agriculture-labs will test the food for viruses and diseases, label every batch with its nutritional value, not relying on values generated by software programs as standard average values that may not represent the actual ones.

The healthcare professionals will promote and educate the people on nutritious food and eating habits to encourage them to maintain a healthier Eco-lifestyle and save the excessive cost of medical treatments.

The nutritionists also work in restaurants and the Eco-city's stores, advising people what to eat and how to cook to preserve the nutritional value of the food for a healthier Eco-lifestyle, in ways that suit different individuals.

As mentioned in *Ecolism 2*, we can modernise farming by using various technologies to produce food throughout the seasons, to get a higher return on investment and make more efficient use of the available lands and funds.

Living a healthy Eco-lifestyle is an obligation in the Eco-city to avoid unnecessary and frequent visits to the doctor asking for medicine to cure minor ailments.

The Eco-nutritionists are the first point of contact to help people eat the right food that suits their bodies and cure minor diseases, by naturally growing specific herbs in their gardens or by getting medicinal tinctures supplied by the hospital's pharmacies as alternative medicine. And they will also encourage people to participate in fitness programmes to reduce the cost of medical services. The Eco-health system will use cheaper and more-efficient alternative medicines to reduce the cost of the Eco-welfare system.

PART 7

Eco-ICT-Councillor

Henri Maalouf declares:

ICT is a colossal extension of the human brain.

Note: Just to avoid confusion in using the terms IT, MIS and ICT, the following explains the meaning of each.

Information technology (IT) is the engineering and functional component of computer networks and systems.

A management information system (MIS) is a computer-based system that provides managers with the tools to efficiently manage an organisation.

Information and communication technologies (ICT) is an extension to IT that integrates telephone, audio and visual telecommunications. For simplicity, I'm using the term ICT or Eco-ICT to describe the computer systems and networks in the Eco-city.

The Eco-ICT-councillor, like every other Eco-councillor, must pass the Eco-criteria-for-selection first, then stand for election and operate in a similar manner to the others, using similar systems and relevant departments, but more suitable for the management of Eco-ICT infrastructure.

The Eco-ICT-councillor must be a subject-matter expert in information technology, hold a master's degree in information systems management or equivalent and must have an outstanding record of accomplishments in developing data centres and end-user IT services.

The Eco-ICT-councillor must be an expert in global competition and the latest technological innovations and advances, along with the threats of hacking/cracking and cyberattacks.

Therefore, the Eco-ICT councillor must ask manufacturers to create unique, customised hardware, specially designed for the Eco-city, free from vulnerabilities and of an unknown design to hackers.

The local software developers must create unique and more-secure operating systems and programming languages for the better prevention of external hacking and cracking attacks. Good examples are Amazon Web Services (AWS) and Microsoft Azure, which are growing exponentially to serve the rest of the world at the most competitive prices.

It is possible to set up similar data centres with additional types of services or set up a joint venture with AWS or Microsoft, considering the purchasing power of one million Eco-homes and the requirements for employees in the Eco-industries, administration and businesses.

The Eco-businesses and Eco-industries will benefit from the Eco-city's large Eco-ICT-data-centres that will host their IT infrastructure and provide their employees with pay-as-you-use virtual desktop computers and standard office applications. The advantages are quick scalability for expansion or contraction as may be required, in addition to the lower cost of secure IT services and 24/7 availability.

In a sizeable Eco-city, the Eco-ICT-data-centre could

become one of the largest in the world, especially when it has the capacity to host IT infrastructure for millions of users. Initially, this will provide for over three million Eco-PCs for one million Eco-homes and another million or more to cover the Eco-businesses, industries, schools, universities and the Eco-city administration. As an added bonus, it could serve many millions nationally and globally.

The Eco-ICT performance increases if we build an ICT university for vocational training to train all the ICT professionals. The software and hardware vendors would have to support the ICT university for their own benefit. They can retrain the unemployed, including young graduates and school leavers, to promote their products and employ them.

Using IT professionals from other countries to manage our IT systems could create risks by exposing our protected data to non-patriotic nationals and put our essential public services at risk of cyberterrorism and cyberattacks.

The Eco-ICT services will have two or more large, scalable Eco-ICT-data-centres to host most types of IT systems and will provide remote access to both small and large businesses, including global organisations, for their applications.

The systems will always be load-balanced between two data centres and will be available 24/7; they will be designed to recover from any failure scenario.

The Eco-ICT-university will train programmers, systems designers and integrators on all types of software and hardware to create a talented pool of young and enthusiastic specialists. The IT experts will be able to compete and accept a lower level of income as one's outgoings in Eco-city are far less than living in other big cities.

The Eco-ICT-data-centres should be environmentally friendly and built underground to benefit from the steady earth temperature at a depth of eight metres, allowing them to consume a lower amount of the energy necessary to cool the hardware.

Above the surface of the underground data centres, there should be highly efficient solar panels and wind-turbine farms to supply the required electricity and store it in a large electric storage system and it should use the national power grid as a backup. This design makes each Eco-ICT-data centre one of the greenest on this planet.

The Eco-programmers may break down and rewrite more-efficient code for every application or create new code to ensure that it is free from bugs and malware that could be embedded by offshore programmers. Rewriting each software application will enable them to provide better technical support for companies.

Global computer software and hardware vendors will run the Eco-ICT-university, training professionals to develop, install, support and sell their products. The trained professionals will develop software applications for the Eco-city's services as well as for other companies to generate income for the Eco-city.

The Eco-ICT-professionals will always share knowledge, complete documentation and give feedback to the Eco-ICT-university, so that they can amend their training programmes and software to suit business requirements.

The ICT security teams will protect the applications and data, complying with the highest Eco-security standards and working practices. The Eco-ICT-security department will enforce the maximum punishment on individuals who betray the trust or confidentiality of their clients or do anything that harms the Eco-city.

The systems' designs will match the most secure banking systems in the world and will become the de-facto standard for each hosted IT system of any company, large or small.

The Eco-ICT will also have call centres, operating at various levels, to meet customers' requests and there will be two types, namely for central and distributed services. The central call centres will be available 24/7, whereas the IT security service will record and monitor the quality of the service. The distributed call centres will be run from the Ecolists' Eco-homes, so that the unemployed can work flexible hours, on an earn-as-you-work basis for each call they answer.

This kind of work is especially suitable for single parents, who can work variable hours and accept a low income, instead of relying upon the Eco-welfare system. And it is equally appropriate for the retired or the physically challenged, as long as they are capable of providing a level of service. It will enable them to feel alive and become productive members of the Eco-society, reducing the burden on the Eco-welfare system.

The Eco-ICT-call-centres will have video-conferencing facilities so that the caller can see the person at the end of the line if required. The incoming calls will be distributed to the relevant groups and the selected Eco-homes, using a telephony hunt group service (if one person does not reply, the call is transferred to another person and whoever answers first gets paid for answering the call). The Eco-homes will have dedicated phone numbers to receive calls and will use free internet voice-over-internet protocol (Eco-VOIP) to reduce the telephone-call costs.

The Eco-ICT-call-centres will create jobs for hundreds of thousands of people and will also generate billions of pounds sterling in revenue to pay back the investment and pay a significant tax to the government. The UK government spends £33 billion annually on ICT projects and the USA spends more than $80 billion, but most firms outsource their ICT overseas and that makes them more vulnerable to cyberattacks, threatens national security and increases local unemployment.

PART 8

Eco-Employment-Councillor

Henri Maalouf declares:

Work smarter, harder and longer to give more to your future and country.

The Eco-employment-councillor, like every other Eco-councillor, must pass the Eco-criteria-for-selection first, then stand for election and operate in a similar manner to the others, using similar systems and relevant departments, but more suitable for Eco-employment and small-business services.

The Eco-employment-councillor must be a subject-matter expert in employment and small businesses, hold a relevant degree in business and must have a successful-enough record of accomplishment in employment or recruitment.

These guidelines are to help with understanding the Eco-employment principles and concepts.

The responsibility of the Eco-employment-councillor is to ensure that the Ecolists are continuously employed and have minimum earnings that match the minimum living standards. *The more people in employment, the less the Eco-welfare system has to subsidise and the more tax they can pay and contribute.*

The more work people do in their earlier days, the more they accumulate equity to live more happily in their retirement.

The ultimate success of the Eco-city's economy is 0% unemployment and 100% productivity throughout the lifespan of each able person. Achieving this goal will determine whether the Eco-employment-councillor remains in office or not or is replaced by a more successful one.

At the time of writing this book, in the year 2017, unemployment in the UK, USA and Germany is less than 5%, while the average in the EU is over 8.5%, rising to 24% in Greece and other EU countries.

Poverty must be eliminated and unemployment must become 0%. Therefore, any person who is able to work should be provided with a job to do. This includes the retired and partly disabled. However, their partial ability and suitability for certain jobs must be matched to increase productivity. Working any number of hours is better than none and doing any job increases their contribution to the society. Consequently, the additional productivity reduces the tax burden on others and compensates for lesser productivity.

The Eco-city's Eco-socio-economic system is designed for any person to work flexible hours at any age. Consequently, this would reduce unemployment to near 0% and increase productivity to near 100%.

Furthermore, in the UK, for example, over 15% of people are inactive or retired, who might live to 84 and most of them are capable of doing easy jobs for at least a few hours a day. They are not included in the unemployment statistics and employing them would increase productivity to 100%, so we should at least give them easy jobs to do while they are capable.

However, it is sometimes difficult to convince locals to take on menial jobs and we still need workers with specific skills.

So, we must hire temporary workers from other countries. Therefore, the most important thing is to prioritise hiring the locals, including training them in the required skills, pressuring them to accept the available jobs and try to keep the employment level as close to 0% as possible.

Increasing the employment percentage and productivity in the Eco-city will also save billions in paying pensions and other allowances.

In the Eco-city, there is no idle time or unemployment, as such. The Ecolists are either working, are in education or are training in the required skills regardless of their age and are contributing to the society as long as they are able.

In the Eco-city, the businesses and industries run 24/7 operations and flexible working hours are available to suit the workers' abilities. Therefore, people can work more when they are younger and continue to work after they retire, even for a few hours a day.

The mother of a new-born child can work flexible hours from home and so can some of the physically challenged, if they have the required abilities or could be trained in them. The Eco-employment system enables the productivity of the Eco-city to reach its highest potential and competitiveness.

The Eco-employment-councillor's responsibility is to find jobs for all the unemployed, including the able retired. It should be a standard process to train the unemployed in the new skills required by the industries. If the Eco-employment system fails to find them a job in the Eco-city, then it must employ them to work in the front-line services till the right job for them become available.

As mentioned earlier in this book, people live on average 84 years and must work as much as possible to reduce the burden on the welfare system and have more money for a better living standard when they get older.

The Eco-city's administration will need security workers of all levels, office administrators, social workers, managers, negotiators, health professionals, chefs, operators and others for all the front-line services. Most of these services can be offered to the unemployed of any age, working flexible hours, until they find the right job or get training in new required skills.

In the West and most parts of the world, we live in upside-down socio-economic systems that give more value to the entertainers than to the educated and highly skilled. The footballer and boxer make more money than the prime minister who runs a country of millions. A footballer kicks a ball and a boxer savagely hits his or her opponent and gets a reward higher than professors. The plumber, electrician and builder make four times more money than a junior doctor or engineer, without the need to have an academic qualification.

A corporate CEO who runs a company earns a bonus that is more than what a prime minister makes in five years of running a country! An MP's salary, excluding their allowances, is less than what an IT specialist or a craftsman receives. And the list goes on, paying more for the less educated and those who have lesser responsibilities than those who are much more accountable.

In the Eco-city, the pay structure is different and corresponds to education, skills, years of experience, quality, productivity, public service and the improvement of the public's lives. Organising the employment and pay structures for the Ecolists into a new Eco-socio-economic system could be challenging.

The first criterion is to balance the minimum income with the minimum outgoings, including inflation, to maintain the Eco-living-standard that is necessary for a dignified life.

The second criterion is to reward success, education and skills development.

The third is that the contribution made during the

productive working years should balance the costs of the Eco-welfare needed during the unproductive years, from birth till death.

The fourth criterion is local jobs for the residents and that profits made from a nation are nationally taxed.

The fifth criterion is training the locals in the required skills.

The sixth criterion is that employment and training are compulsory if a person has an outstanding mortgage or debts.

The seventh criterion is that the Eco-employment-councillor has the responsibility to employ the unemployed or train them in the required skills.

The eighth criterion is to ensure that people get paid according to the value of their work regardless of their sex or origin.

The ninth criterion is protecting the interests of the employee and the employer for mutual benefits.

And the list goes on to a fairer social structure that is more organised, balanced and has absolute equality between sexes, races and all classes of the society. It is always the government's responsibility to ensure justice and fairness.

The Eco-employment-councillor should encourage people to work harder, faster, smarter and longer; to accept less and to compete with the rising East and the rest of the world to maintain Eco-employment's competitiveness and sustainability.

The South Koreans work an average of 2,200 hours a year, as some Chinese do, while the UK's workers work 1,600 hours a year. In India, there is no fixed concept of working time. Whenever and wherever there is a job to carry out, the workers keep working, learning on the job and asking others for help until the job is completed.

Even in some eastern European countries, the salaries are a quarter of the British minimum wage and they are hard workers, skilled and educated. But their cost of living is much lower, so they can afford to survive on lower wages.

Therefore, in the Eco-city, the outgoings are kept to a minimum, which means people can afford to live on a lower income, give employers substantial value for money and be very competitive by applying the best of international employment systems.

Eco-Self-Employment

Henri Maalouf declares:

If no one employs me, I employ myself.

The self-employed typically work countless hours, including weekends and holidays. Their incentive is to get the job done and earn a decent living.

In the Eco-city, the Eco-businesses will allow anyone to run his or her own business from home. The Eco-homes have a high-speed internet connection and the facility to access all the necessary business applications through the Eco-ICT-data-centres.

The Eco-home is designed as open space, with three bedrooms and may have a basement to use as a business office or for running licensed craft or experimental innovation. The Eco-businesses' practices will provide the flexibility for single parents, people with physical disabilities and the semi-retired elderly to have adequate facilities to work.

The design of the Eco-city and Eco-homes will enable people to become extremely competitive because of the low overheads of working from home. The Eco-commercial-bank will help small businesses with a low-interest, controlled overdraft facility so that they do not spend more than necessary to avoid loss and bankruptcy. Eco-business education and advice will be available to give small businesses the right guidance and help to succeed.

Helping mothers and lone parents to gain a footing in business is also essential for boosting the economy. Some efficacious mothers worked from home and began with a £500 investment and now are producing £7 billion for the economy.

Personally, I had a £5,000 overdraft facility in 1990 and used to build computers and sell them as a small business. My turnover was £200,000 a year. But, a few years later, the banking systems changed and I was unable to continue because I could not get an overdraft facility; what made things worse was the credit-scoring system that is very restrictive, unforgiving and detrimental to small businesses.

In the Eco-city, the Eco-employment-councillor encourages all the unemployed individuals to set up their own Eco-business and will help them with access to the Eco-city's business centre, industries and agriculture to sell their products outside the Eco-city and to the rest of the world.

The small businesses can convert most of the unemployed into self-employed workers and turn hundreds of thousands into income generators, instead of being consumers of the Eco-welfare budget.

Eco-Competitiveness and Eco-Productivity

Balance your outgoings with your incomings; work smarter, longer and harder to serve your country; and compete with the East and West.

The cost of living in the West is extremely high because of

the demanding and luxurious lifestyles. The Western socio-economic systems and commercial pressures tempt consumers into spending more than they earn to purchase unnecessary and unaffordable luxuries.

In the Eco-city, the pressure will be the opposite by encouraging people to live within their means, live better, spend less and accept any job required to survive or retrain in new required skills, so as to be able to sustain the Eco-socio-economic system and compete with the rest of the world's overgrowing population.

The British are 30% less productive than the Germans, 20% less than the Americans and 18% behind the French, not to mention the Koreans, Indians, Japanese, Chinese and others. Therefore, it is the duty of the Ecolists to work smarter, harder and longer to stand a chance of survival against the others. They must become more competitive and give the investors higher value for their investment to lower the overheads and sustain their services.

One of my experiences when I worked for the Swedish company Ericsson 40 years ago, was that they test their employees for specialisation aptitude, selecting the fastest and most accurate person who can do the job quickly without mistakes.

This aptitude test is a compulsory requirement of the Eco-workers in the Eco-city and is a measure of their ability to give good value for money. I hope they can compete with the Germans, Koreans, Indians and all the others.

There is a conflict of interest between the businesses pushing a globalisation agenda, while the national interest is pushing back for protectionism. If globalisation wins, that will create local unemployment and the national governments will pay for it, while if protectionism wins, then businesses must operate with lower profits. Therefore, a solution must be found to satisfy both interests as it is in the design of this Eco-city and Eco-socio-economic system.

To elaborate further, let's assume an example based on £2,000/month wages for a particular skill paid to a national worker compared with £1,000/month paid to a non-national worker. A business prefers to pay the non-national employees £1,000/month, to reduce overheads, become more competitive and make more profits.

In this case, the national worker becomes unemployed and the government must pay about £1,000/month in social care and welfare benefits. It gets worse when the unemployed locals resort to violence, drugs and anti-social behaviour that harms the society, because they have no income.

However, when the local becomes more competitive, accepting £1,000/month because the cost of living is lower and the government subsidises the business with a tax-free margin, then the company will hire locals and it becomes a win-win situation.

In the Eco-city, the cost of living for the worker is 50% less, the overhead for the business is also about 50% less and the tax-free margin guarantees that there is no loss for the investment, so everybody will be better off.

PART 9

Eco-Education-Councillor

Henri Maalouf declares:

*The more you know, the further you go and, with the right
skill, you get the job at the mill.*

The Eco-education-councillor, like the rest, must pass the Eco-
criteria-for-selection first, then stand for election and operate
in a similar manner to the others, using the Eco-systems and
appropriate departments that are more suitable for education
and lifetime training, so that anyone may learn new skills, adapt
to the advances in technologies and adapt to available jobs.

The Eco-education-councillor must have a degree in
teaching and extensive experience as a headteacher of a school
or university to understand education better than a politician.

These guidelines are to help with understanding the Eco-
education principles and concepts.

The responsibility of the Eco-education-councillor is
to ensure that the Ecolists can get free education for life and
training in new skills at any time they wish or if they must have
specific skills to get a particular job.

The Eco-education-councillor must coordinate with the

businesses and industries to understand the skills required and give feedback to schools, universities and training centres to run courses for the industries' required skills.

The Eco-city's Eco-socio-economic system operates as a cost-effective and good-value-for-money Eco-lifestyle. *The current education and vocational training systems are expensive and not affordable for everyone.* However, online training for soft skills is very cheap and affordable for anyone.

Let us take an example: students who go to university to learn computer science for three or four years pay about £14,000 a year, including accommodation and other expenses. Eventually, they get a degree in computer science and can hardly find a job that is relevant to their qualification. The alternative is to learn online using the internet for one of the software vendor's certifications in six months or less and get a skilled job easily. It used to be expensive, costing a few thousand for a one or two-week course.

However, in recent days, online internet training is advancing and increasingly converting physical school classes to virtual ones. It has become much cheaper for students to learn any subject they like from £10/month. The students could complete multiple-choice or scenario-type questions with an authorised test centre and get the results instantly online. After they qualify for a relevant certification, they can work and earn more than £64k a year in a permanent job or get £500/day as contractors, after long experience.

Personally, at the age of 66, I learned AWS internet cloud certification for £12 and got a suitable job that pays £500/day, but I do possess previous IT experience and other similar qualifications, that made it easier for me to learn the newer technology.

One might ask, how can a trainer or online school do it?

Well, it is easy. He or she sets up the video course material with access to a virtual lab over the internet and about 30,000 students worldwide pay for the same course, with the potential for 100,000 students or more to pay the small subscription fee. Compare paying £12 and learning from home to paying £14,000.

Even the trainer or teacher makes much more money by writing these courses and publishing them online for hundreds of thousands of students. Instead of the teacher getting £35,000/year, for example, he/she can get £12 x 100,000 = £1.2 million.

There is no reason why the Eco-city could not set up such systems to educate the Ecolists for free, sell the courses online to the rest of the world, generate income to cover the costs and make a profit.

Education and continuous skills training are permanent companions that follow us, like our guardian angel, from the cradle to the grave. The more we nourish them, the better we become. It is our weapon in the battle for survival in a competitive world.

The Eco-city's academic and vocational education will remain free as part of the Eco-welfare system for the greater good of all. The education and skills specialisations are becoming more demanding, sophisticated and innovative and newer technologies will keep forcing new skills requirements.

The modern trend and concept for educating learners is to abolish physical classrooms and replace them with virtual internet ones, unless there is a need for interacting with machines or lab equipment. Therefore, students can learn from home, meet classmates and the teachers online using the Eco-PC and webcam as a video-conferencing system. Students can relisten to the recordings of lessons and ask questions on relevant forums where students and educators exchange knowledge.

This system will offer the rest of the world affordable

education for most online learning subjects. An Eco-city may not cover all ranges of new skills and specialisations, but it will undoubtedly include the main categories of science, technology and vocational skills to match the requirements of the Eco-businesses and Eco-industries.

To elaborate further, let us take an example of the science of herpetology, which is a branch of zoology dealing with reptiles and amphibians. The Eco-city might be able to get a professor to teach the subject or to communicate remotely online from another country, but might not have a job for a graduate in the subject, nor an amphibian habitat for scientific observations and experimentation. Therefore, trips to a natural habitat can be arranged by the Eco-city's education system. Likewise, just as another example, the Eco-city may not have a Large Hadron Collider for scientific research on physics particles or a large space-research centre like the National Aeronautics and Space Administration (NASA). Therefore, the Eco-city will educate as much as possible and help its Ecolists to pursue their advanced education and careers elsewhere.

The Eco-city is designed to be self-sufficient and sustainable. Therefore, the emphasis is to educate and train the Ecolists in the required skills for the available jobs. But this does not mean Eco-education will stop students from learning specialisations that have no future in the Eco-city. The students can be guided to study a subject that guarantees a job in the Eco-city. Otherwise, they can follow their dreams outside the Eco-city.

Promoting home studying can also be supported by the Eco-city with educational TV programmes and an Eco-Open-University channel running a variety of courses, where a student can watch and learn, download the recording to review, email questions, join forums and get answers.

The manufacturers, ICT software vendors and businesses

may also run training courses on skills to match their products' requirements and employ specialists or influence universities to train in skills for the required jobs.

In 1988, I studied advanced microprocessor technology (AMT) hoping that I could get a job in computers afterwards. I was disappointed to discover that what I had studied was not compatible with the market requirements for an IT profession and I had to study again to obtain vendor's certifications such as a Microsoft Certified Systems Engineer (MCSE) and Citrix Certified Enterprise Administrator (CCEA), plus many other courses to quickly get a job and make more money than I would have if I had worked as an electronic engineer.

The Eco-city's Eco-socio-economic system allows people to work flexible hours in industries and businesses operating 24/7, which helps people work a few hours to raise their income and study or train for the remaining hours of the day to improve their skills.

In the Eco-city, there will be different teaching programmes to suit infants, toddlers, pre-schoolers and school-aged students; then there will be options for vocational training, colleges or universities. The education system in an Eco-city allows parents to teach and take care of their children while working flexible hours from home.

It must be compulsory that the education and skills' training remain free, available for everyone, financed by the Eco-city and run by appropriate teachers, not administrators.

Eco-education may not impose expensive school trips, due to their prohibitive costs and may not allow inset days and school breaks, to enable students to study more as a full-time job would be, except for short breaks during Christmas and the summer for one month a year maximum. A nutritious school breakfast, lunch and dinner will be provided for free, to ensure healthier and smarter children and to give the parents more time to work and not have to worry about cooking for their children.

The students may stay at school after teaching hours to do their homework and teachers will assist them and explain the subject or the question if they did not understand it the first time, to ensure a higher rate of success.

A General Certificate of Secondary Education (GCSE) in the UK or a high-school failure in other countries will result in retaking the exam until success is achieved. Otherwise, an aptitude test must be taken to assess the suitability for learning a profession at a vocational training centre. If all fails, the alternative is to learn on the job in a factory or a business.

As an example, in the UK, there is a celebrity called Simon Cowell, a reality television talent judge, producer and entrepreneur. He is known on the British and American TV talent competition shows of *Pop Idol*, *X Factor* and *Britain's/ America's Got Talent*. Simon left school with just General Certificates of Education (GCEs or O levels) in English language and literature and then attended technical college where he gained another GCE in sociology. However, he needed no academic or professional qualifications to succeed in life and is now worth half a billion dollars.

I am not favouring or encouraging people to take the easy path and achieve celebrity status in entertainment, sport or entrepreneurship without education. The real respect will always be for educated people and especially scientists for their work to improve our civilisations.

PART 10

Eco-Health-Councillor

Henri Maalouf declares:

If a disease is genetic, cure it; if not, prevent it.

The Eco-health-councillor should be an experienced medical doctor or professor who will be able to manage the health service better than a politician.

The Eco-health-councillor, like every other Eco-councillor, must pass the Eco-criteria-for-selection first, then stand for election and operate in an equivalent manner to the others and create departments suitable for health issues and the wellbeing of the Ecolists.

The following guidelines are to help with understanding the Eco-health principles and concepts.

The prime responsibility of the Eco-health-councillor is to ensure that the Ecolists follow a healthy lifestyle to remain disease-free and save on the cost of medical treatment.

The Eco-city's clinics will use efficient methods to reduce the physician's consultation time. For example, the Ecolists will access their patient records online, select the appropriate ailment questionnaire, answer the questions as much as possible and submit it online.

Also, a video-conference call can be established if further diagnosis is essential for a more accurate prognosis. If blood or other tests are required, the results should be provided in a short period, while the patient is waiting. Also, the medicine must be prescribed and given to the patient all in one visit.

Although medical care would be free for the unemployed and retired, it could be chargeable for those who can afford it, depending on the Eco-city's health budget. The medical staff or administrators must upload all the patient's medical records to the Eco-city's website and make it accessible for each patient to download and store on their ECDL card.

The Eco-medical system can host services for people outside the Eco-city to generate income, but will be entirely independent and available if doctors have idle time. Otherwise, more physicians and nurses will be hired to do such a commercial job.

The Eco-lifestyle in the Eco-city should have no environmental factors or kinds of contaminated food that weaken the immune system and cause any diseases. To elaborate further, to give a few examples of what I mean and to enlighten most of the public about such causes, please read the following to get an idea of what is going on in our civilisation.

My sister was hit by cancer. Although she always had medical tests and went for check-ups, ate moderately, preserved the shape of her body and had always been in good health, still cancer attacked her. I asked her oncologist how it developed and what caused it. He said: "If you create the environment for it to grow, it will; if you expose the body to radiation, it will affect it; and if you eat contaminated food without knowing what it contains, some chemicals will trigger it. The cancer cells will grow and attack if they are not detected at earlier stages and become difficult to cure."

Also, there is a hereditary factor that varies in percentages from one person to another, which might cause cancer to develop if the immune system is weak. Additionally, it may be caused by exposure to environmental radiation, which may come from the ultraviolet (UV) radiation of the sun or nuclear waste that is not buried properly.

Environmental pollution does not only cause cancer but many other diseases. This makes a case for building Eco-cities and people living an Eco-lifestyle, as discussed throughout the Ecolism books. Mainly, this is eating fresh food from the Eco-city without genetic modification (no GM food) and that is not imported from unknown sources, canned or sprayed with harmful insecticides. The food should be naturally and organically grown and preferably eaten in its growing seasons.

Apparently, eating in moderation a sensible diet to suit one's body is a significant factor in health and wellbeing. Living happily; engaging in exercise, sex or social activities; plus listening to music, are also vital for healthier living.

Sometimes eating herbs improves the immune system and prevents minor ailments or diseases in the long term. However, if the alternative medicine and proper diet fail, then doctors must resort to synthetic medication, which should be wisely selected to avoid its side effects and should be stopped as soon as it is not needed. And if things get out of hand, then a surgical procedure may become necessary as a last resort.

The Eco-city must have hospitals for severe conditions, equipped with labs, all the necessary instruments, scanners, operation rooms and other necessities. The doctors must be trustworthy, respect the patient's confidentiality when necessary and adhere to the Hippocratic Oath. And if a doctor fails to do what is right, then he/she will be rehabilitated like everyone else and in cases of severe or deliberate misconduct will be expelled from the Eco-city after losing all of his/her equity.

It is always essential to detect a developing disease in its earlier stages for easier treatment. Therefore, it should be compulsory for every Ecolist to have a general check-up and other health screening tests, periodically, for the rapid detection of diseases and to prevent consequential expensive treatments.

The accident and emergency (A&E) service could be a walk-in service or by calling an ambulance for severe cases. The ambulance service will come with a junior doctor to try to cure the person on site or refer them to an A&E senior doctor or surgeon for further treatment when necessary.

In the Eco-city, the hospitals are in its centre, so it makes sense to build clinics in the proximity to the elderly who live at the perimeter of the Eco-city and are more likely to need urgent medical care.

PART 11

Eco-Entertainment-Councillor

Henri Maalouf declares:

Life without happiness is like a body without a soul and like a stagnant robot without an electric charge.

The Eco-entertainment councillor, like every one of his/ her colleagues, must adhere to the Eco-criteria-for-selection first, before qualifying to stand for election and operate in a similar manner to the rest, using comparable systems and relevant departments, but more suitable for entertainment.

The Eco-entertainment-councillor must have a good track record in managing large entertainment resorts, such as Disneyland or others.

The following guidelines are to help with understanding the Eco-entertainment principles and concepts.

Life is a cycle with interdependent components to keep it going. Food provides the necessary energy to keep the body alive, light is needed for most plants to grow, darkness is essential to cultivate mushrooms and it is vital for human beings to sleep and rest. It is not plausible to live like programmed robots, work 24/7, never sleep, have no feelings of beauty or love and no sense of happiness.

All of us must work to survive, rest to revitalise and have enough energy to work again. But we also need the motivation and the triggers to keep our cycle of life running. Like the heart's electrical impulses keep it beating, we also need entertainment. Likewise, fuel is necessary for a vehicle to run and happiness, pleasure, fun, love and sex are required for our bodies and souls to keep going and be motivated to continue living the cycle of life with higher productivity.

In an Eco-city, we must all have civilised entertainment activities to provide happiness and harmony for the Ecolists and the Eco-city visitors. The Eco-entertainment-councillor does not allow savage and harmful sports, such as boxing and fox hunting. Such sports are not civilised ones and are closer to medieval times when fighting and killing in the arena was a form of entertainment.

Even some football rules allow for ferocious tackles and cause injury for the players, like sliding in front of the players to kick the ball, which causes the opponent to fall and getting injured because of pushing or overtaking to get the ball. Some games are more business-orientated than being an entertaining national sport and international competition.

Some sports competitors, especially footballers, have no patriotism or loyalty to a national team. They can be purchased by the highest bidders. Eco-sport and Eco-entertainment must be free, cheap or at cost price, not a profiteering business.

In the Eco-city, all physical and mental games are encouraged, as long as no harm or injury to anyone would result from a confrontational match. Competitions should be friendly games and Eco-awards given to the winners.

The Eco-entertainment-councillor encourages non-violent sports and fun activities, such as music concerts, singing contests, musical acts and comedy. People from outside the Eco-city may be invited to cover the costs or generate extra income for developing the entertainment skills and arts. Roller coasters and scary thrill rides are excellent stimulation, which increase excitement and cause an adrenalin rush for healthy individuals and generate income to cover the investment.

The Eco-entertainment-councillor encourages games like *Ninja Warrior* or *Gladiators* that motivate competitors to improve their agility, speed and physical strength. Also, mental games such as chess, mazes and puzzles to enhance mental abilities are promoted. Perhaps, in time, the Eco-city could build many stadiums for various sports' activities and competitions in addition to resort parks similar to Disneyland.

The Eco-city's perimeter main road may hold electric car races and carnivals, in addition to marathon activities as a weekly competition for people to run around the Eco-city.

Gambling for money should not be allowed in the Eco-city. However, people can play card games or even bingo to stimulate their ego by winning or trying to win, but not for money or even virtual credit or any equivalent value. The reward for winning in any game or sport can be registered as scoring points and those who gather the most points can participate in an annual championship for national or international competitions.

PART 12

Eco-Transport-Councillor and Eco-Infrastructure-Councillor

Henri Maalouf declares:

Birds roam free and so should we.

The Eco-transport-councillor and Eco-infrastructure-councillor do not differ from other Eco-councillors in general function and must go through the Eco-criteria-for-selection before being elected and work like the others, but using comparable systems and relevant departments more suitable for the transport and infrastructure disciplines.

He or she must be at least an electromechanical engineer and is assisted by a team of architects experienced in planning the development of a large city.

The following guidelines are to help with understanding the Eco-transport and Eco-infrastructure principles and concepts.

Initially, before we build an Eco-city, we need to prepare its infrastructure to suit the Eco-homes and the sustenance areas.

The Eco-homes need amenities such as water, electricity, solar panels, edible gardens and high-speed fibre-optic cable connectivity for TV channels, phones and internet access. Apart from the roads, the inhabitants need schools, hospitals, places to work and front-line services. The emphasis of the primary infrastructure is to build an Eco-city that is self-sufficient and has sustainable systems.

The planning should be long-term and cover every future eventuality. Therefore, if an Eco-city has one million Eco-homes, each must be built for future expansion with the possibility of building two floors on top. Consequently, the roads and the rest of the infrastructure must be adequate for 12 million inhabitants instead of four million and be ready for any expansion without restructuring.

The planning must include every detail such as the fibre-optic cable that supplies the TV, computer network and the internet, which should be designed to withstand a larger capacity and could provide an excess for future expansion requirements. This is similar for the water, electricity backup and the roads. The roads should be large enough for over four million cars all driving to work simultaneously with limited speed. But, ideally, the Eco-socio-economic system should favour the use of public transport, such as trains and buses or using cycles for shorter distances. The supply trenches or tunnels across the Eco-city should be separate from the roads so any possible maintenance or expansion installations can be completed without disturbing the traffic.

The water-drainage system that takes the water away from the Eco-city's roads should be big enough not to flood under the most extreme weather. The Eco-city's constructed river should not flood either and should be designed not to take in sand or mud, but if it is not avoidable, then it should be regularly dredged without harming the fish.

The Eco-sustenance area also needs planning for the infrastructure of the industries, businesses, agriculture, energy, water sections and others. Additionally, the Eco-centre and the surrounding administration buildings need planning too.

The Eco-transport vehicles in the Eco-city must be electric trains, buses, cars, scooters, e-bikes, bamboo bikes or any other electric vehicle that the Eco-city will manufacture locally. The trains will travel across the Eco-city, from east to west and north to south, passing through the centre, while the buses will transport passengers from the streets to the train stops.

The Eco-industries and Eco-businesses can use smaller buses to transport their employees to their premises from the Eco-city's perimeter gates. But, some people may be able to afford to use motorised bikes or autonomous cars to commute to their destination.

The transport in the Eco-city is to be provided free, to help the Ecolists commuting to work, schools, universities, hospitals and the rest of the Eco-city facilities, such as the Eco-restaurants and Eco-leisure-centres.

The Eco-city will produce enough electricity to run all the transport vehicles and will install electric charging stations at convenient locations. The main roads will have five lanes; each will have permanent road markings to guide the autonomous cars for safer driving and so there will be no chance for an accident to happen and the design must comply with the Eco-safety standards.

The Eco-city will try to convince car manufacturers such as Tesla or Jaguar to have a branch in the Eco-industry section, to manufacture the best Eco-electric-vehicles and be in charge of electric buses, bikes, scooters, trains, etc.

Safety in the Eco-city is paramount. Therefore, the Eco-electric-vehicles must be assisted by all kinds of sensors to stop the vehicle from colliding with other objects. The roads in the Eco-city will be designed with lanes that support the vehicle's sensors and the driver should be able to override the sensors if they fail to function correctly.

The autonomous or driver-less car will automatically stop when it approaches an object, at a safe distance that corresponds to its speed and the lanes will have roadside protection to isolate and protect the bike tracks, preventing any fatality from an accidental collision.

Scooters for the disabled will be mainly used at the Eco-city's outer perimeter and will be driven on specially marked lanes on the pavement, which are also separate from the bike tracks and roads for cars. The trees and berry bushes planted on both sides of the roads will also provide a soft fence to dampen any collision.

The transport infrastructure must provide an efficient system for over two million people to work in the Eco-city's surrounding industries and must be free of charge. But it must also be scalable and adaptable for the possible population growth and their requirements.

PART 13

Eco-Justice-Councillor

Henri Maalouf declares:

Justice is not for the rich or poor, for one race or colour or applied to one more than the other; it should be equal for all, great or small.

The Eco-justice-councillor, like every other Eco-councillor, must pass the Eco-criteria-for-selection first, then stand for election and operate in a similar manner to the others, using similar systems and relevant departments, but more suitable for justice, freedom, ethics and equality.

The Eco-justice-councillor must have a PhD in law and preferably be a retired judge with extensive experience. An Eco-justice-councillor must not succumb to bribes, surrender to political pressures or other influences and must always be impartial irrespective of whoever is involved in a case.

In our Western world, the justice system is overregulated, complicated, imperfect, illogically contradicting the purpose of the laws and is becoming vaguer. *The statutes and judgments are like a central circle surrounded by multiple roads leading in various directions and sometimes loops around itself with no clear answer to a case.*

The laws should be one road with opposite ends leading in opposite directions only. If a judge is ethical, independent and has common sense, then there will be less need for a myriad of unnecessary, sophisticated and convoluted laws. This is because the judge should rely on high principles and the purpose of the law, rather than its literal interpretation or similar cases referenced as precedencies that may override the purpose of the law itself.

The wealthy can afford expensive and outstanding law firms capable of circumventing the law, interpreting the wording of the syntax differently and prolonging the case to become unaffordable for the impoverished, who consequently lose in most cases unless there is a public outcry and media spin.

It is prudent for an Eco-city to run a free Eco-mediation service, instead of referring offenders to the traditional, expensive national justice system. Although the national courts have the final say in financial penalties and prison sentences, the Eco-mediation service tries to find the truth, collect the evidence and rehabilitate offenders instead of imprisoning them.

The rationale behind such mediation in the form of Eco-courts is because traditional lawsuits are costly, time-consuming and becoming increasingly unaffordable for the destitute living on a low income, who sometimes do not even have access to legal aid or understands his/her rights. In most instances, traditional courts are less efficient and cases may drag on for years.

The Eco-Justice System

Henri Maalouf declares:

A vague law is not a just law and without a defined ethical purpose, it is subject to vagueness.

The Eco-city has its Eco-courts that are run in a different way than the traditional ones to make them efficient, equipped with comprehensive scrutiny and provide a quick final judgment with no appeal. The way the Eco-court system works in the Eco-city is to remove the tradition of appointing a solicitor for the claimant and another for the defendant. Both solicitors, along with one or more judges, a subject-matter expert and a psychologist become an Eco-jury for the verdict and final judgment. It is unlike the traditional jury of 12 members randomly selected from members of the public who do not have the expertise to judge in complex cases. The number and type of the Eco-jury depend on the seriousness of the matter and its required experts.

The following paragraphs are a simple illustration of the Eco-justice system's concept and, eventually, it will be up to the judges to set the laws. It briefly shows an example of each of three categories: Eco-criminal, Eco-commercial and Eco-tort courts. Furthermore, in the next part of this book, there are further examples of some principles as guidance for the local Eco-laws and in the next book *Ecolism 2*, there will be more details. Eventually, these laws evolve and the judges add to them as needed by the Ecolists and the Eco-city's sectors.

The Eco-Criminal Court

Henri Maalouf declares:

> *The crime of murdering one person is equivalent to causing misery and injustice for a society.*

The Eco-criminal laws cover major crimes committed by any individual, including those in civil or public authorities. Major crimes are considered to be killing of any type, paedophilia, treachery, industrial espionage, misleading or infringing human rights, even by governors.

The seriousness of a criminal offence determines the level of the Eco-jury required and the kind of penalty applied. In more severe cases, three judges, a prosecutor, two solicitors, a psychologist, experts in matters relevant to the case, reliable witnesses and others might be required. In less-severe cases, a judge and security officer may be adequate.

The Eco-Commercial Court

The Eco-commercial laws cover companies, consumers, banking, employment and any issues related to businesses inside or outside the Eco-city.

The Eco-commercial jury is different from the one for the Eco-criminal court. As usual, there would be a judge for small cases and more people for more serious ones. The small-cases jury will resolve the disputes among small businesses, employees and consumers. But for greater disputes, the Eco-jury consists of two Eco-judges or more, Eco-solicitors, an Eco-prosecutor and may include a head of an Eco-committee and/or Eco-councillor. (The Eco-committees are described in the Eco-governance part of this book. It is a tripartite system consisting of committees that are representative of specialised Eco-councillors, businesses and the public.) If there is a deadlock in a case or a lack of applicable or disputed laws, the Eco-mayor or Eco-supreme-judge will have the final say and judge the matter guided by the Eco-city's welfare systems and the purposes of its laws.

The rationale behind involving the Eco-committees is to balance the conflict of interests among the consumers, workforce, businesses and governance. This is because the underlying objective of the Eco-commercial laws is to create protective economic policies that will guard and regulate a harmonious relationship between business and the Eco-city. One part of the commercial laws is to protect the Eco-city from businesses' misconduct and failure to run a successful, ethical business. The other aims are to protect investors in the Eco-city from external competitors, aggressive takeovers, industrial espionage and resolve internal disputes between companies and the Eco-city.

Protecting the businesses from failure includes scrutinising or prosecuting CEOs and managers for mismanagement and the inability to make an industry or a company profitable. The failure of an enterprise affects the workforce, causing unemployment that results in a higher burden on the taxpayers and the Eco-welfare system.

Another part of the commercial policies is to provide protection from unfair unilateral or multilateral international agreements. The balance should always be maintained, taking into consideration the protection of the Eco-industries and Eco-businesses.

For example, a trade agreement between the USA and the EU on car tariffs is unbalanced. The EU imposes a 10% tariff on US-manufactured cars, while the US imposes a 2.5% tariff on the EU-manufactured cars. This sort of imbalance does not protect the US car manufacturers from fierce competition from their EU counterparts. Therefore, protecting the Eco-industries comes first and trading on the basis of win-win business deals comes second. The provision for changing the terms of any agreement when circumstances change should be included to maintain the balance of mutual benefits.

An example of consumer protection is the interface between

the providers of products and services and their customers. The principle is to protect David from Goliath. In other words, protecting the weak from the powerful. It is not good enough to say customers must comply with the suppliers' terms and conditions or they cannot receive such services or products. The reality is that some services or products are essential necessities for a decent living standard or survival. Therefore, this must be regulated by the Eco-justice system and all agreements must be standard templates written by judges.

To elaborate further, the daily necessities such as water, electricity, internet access, food, necessary clothes, transport, healthcare, welfare system, justice, communication means, accommodation and anything else that is essential to our minimum living standard should be either free or regulated by the Eco-city.

The Eco-Tort Court

The Eco-tort court is similar to other courts, but on a lower scale and more rehabilitative than penalising in nature.

The Eco-tort law is for all small cases among individuals and mainly can be solved by mediation or results in educational rehabilitation. The Eco-tort court should have a psychologist trying to find a solution to a problem between two individuals, who will advise on a course of action, either educational programmes or rehabilitation. The judge will order the course of action to be implemented. Otherwise, reoccurrence of the same dispute leads to a financial penalty and a more-severe rehabilitation programme that includes isolation.

Another role the psychologist is to recommend improvements in the Eco-socio-economic system to remove the causes that create such disputes between individuals, families, friends or Ecolists. Educational programmes could be devised to prevent such anti-social behaviour and non-harmonious social interactions among the Ecolists.

The Eco-principles are the guidelines for every Ecolist to follow and comply with, as well as guidance for the laws. Eco-rehab is the corrective measure to deter and prevent the reoccurrence of offences. The Eco-city does not believe in prison sentences, because even if it hinders criminal behaviour, it does not re-educate and correct human genetics or acquired behaviour. Prisons do not guarantee the prevention of repeat offences. The evidence is that the number of prisoners keeps rising and our civilisation is not becoming free from human crimes yet.

The Eco-Justice System

The Eco-justice system must be defined and structured to avoid the flaws in any current justice system in the 21st century. The following paragraphs outline the structure of the Eco-justice system.

Eco-Prosecution

Eco-prosecution, in all types of courts, can use any ethical procedures and means to examine the parties involved to ascertain the truth. The means used should be supervised by both solicitors, a psychologist and a judge. This might include advanced polygraph devices, psychological analysis, truth pills, reliable or genuine witnesses and evidence from the Eco-security services to assist in ascertaining the truth. The claimant and defendant have no right to keep quiet and must answer the questions truthfully and explain the reasons for his/her actions.

The Eco-Jury

The Eco-jury consists of one or more Eco-judges, two Eco-solicitors both collecting facts from the defendant and claimant but not defending either of them, an Eco-prosecutor, an Eco-psychologist and subject-matter experts. Their role is to establish the truth and whether there is compliance with the Eco-principles. They will publicly interrogate the accused or the parties involved in a case and broadcast it on the Eco-city's website for transparency and for lessons to be learned from incidents. The roles of the Eco-psychologist and Eco-judge are to detect the lies, determine the necessary rehabilitation measures and feedback to the Eco-councillors to improve the Eco-socio-economic system to try to eliminate the root causes and prevent the reoccurrence of offences.

Eco-Punishment

The Eco-punishment system is based on the Eco-principles and virtues that override any technicalities of the laws and are based on rehabilitation rather than penalties in the form of prison sentences. It does not penalise offenders using simple imprisonment in lockable cells for most offences, unless the offender is deranged. This system is suggested to eradicate the existing, harsh and yet unhelpful system of penalisation. Instead, it advocates rehabilitation and correcting the cause of the action or crime. Therefore, a judgment will include directives to the Eco-councillors to check their Eco-socio-economic systems and rules to remedy the underlying causes of such offences when a pattern occurs.

Once the truth has been ascertained and the offender has been found guilty, then the judge orders a proper rehabilitation programme or a financial-penalty judgment or both. If the offence is beyond the Eco-justice system's capability or jurisdiction, then the offender will be handed over to the national authorities for further prosecution by the laws of the land, accompanied by the Eco-court's recommendations.

The Ecolists may not have the finances to pay the monetary penalty or enough income to pay in instalments, but they might have equity in their Eco-home. Therefore, the financial penalty could reduce their savings or leave them with negative equity. The consequences will force them to work harder and longer to compensate for the loss, making them more productive and in the hope that it will deter them from repeating an offence.

The Eco-punishment system resorts to reconditioning treatment and not prisons to reform the undesired behaviour, prevent reoccurrence and discipline the Eco-society. If someone made a mistake, lost their temper, did not have self-control or was just unaware of what is wrong and what is right, then re-educational and mental treatments are the best options for the correction needed to transform the person into being virtuous.

However, sometimes, more-intensive psychiatric treatments are necessary to stop the repetition of offences. These matters will be left to psychologists to determine the best course of action and rehabilitation programmes. Sometimes, there are social, educational or socio-economic factors that create the root causes influencing human behaviour. In these cases, the social repercussions must be removed and corrected and the offender re-educated to adapt to the desired and utopian Eco-social harmony.

There is a saying 'prevention is better than cure' and, similarly, remove the root causes rather than using incarceration and instead of blaming the offender, blame the socio-economic system for failing to set up the ideal social environment.

Eco-Rehab

The Eco-city's justice system replaces prisons with rehabilitation centres to correct what has gone wrong in a human's behaviour and study the root causes to provide feedback to the Eco-socio-economic system so that what caused the offence to occur may be amended. Some wrongdoings are mild and can be treated more easily than others. And some crimes might be due to a long history of addiction, wrong social upbringing or solely a genetic mental disorder they have had since birth. In any case, the Eco-psychiatrists will endure until they find a cure, re-educate to rejuvenate and keep the Eco-society safe from offenders.

As in health, where prevention is better than cure, it is the same in social conduct; we must remove the causes that wither the roses.

There are those who step over the line, get out of control and ignore the Eco-rules of responsible freedom, equality, independence and ethics. In such cases, re-education becomes a necessity as the first course of action, followed by total isolation or expulsion from the Eco-society, to sustain social harmony, until comprehensive reform occurs.

If religion causes animosity and hatred of others, it is best for that religion to not exist. If a preacher of a religion influences believers to disturb the peace, freedom and harmonious living with others, then that preacher must be re-educated or removed and stopped from negatively influencing followers and causing harm to the society.

Financial institutions and politicians should also be stopped from harming society through misconduct and abusing their powers. They should be re-educated or have those powers removed.

Eco-Security

Henri Maalouf declares:

Do not allow the thief to enter then blame him for stealing.

Eco-security is part of the Eco-justice system designed to protect the Eco-city, collect information and evidence about any misconduct. The Eco-security personnel must be all vetted. It is preferable if they have experience as soldiers or police officers and also must have clean criminal records. However, there are many types of Eco-security teams and many skills are required, so, for certain tasks, experience is unnecessary and training should be provided.

Eco-security is paramount in the Eco-city to monitor, control and manage every concern that threatens the peace and harmony among the inhabitants, industries, businesses and the Eco-council. Every member of the Eco-society must be vigilant and aid Eco-security to preserve the stability of the Eco-socio-economic system.

The Eco-city has zero tolerance for offences, misconduct and anything else that disturbs its harmony. Therefore, its Eco-security teams have the authority to remove an Eco-councillor from power or remove a CEO of a company upon misconduct or an offence, if an Eco-judge orders them to do so.

The Eco-security teams may temporarily employ anyone who is unemployed, who can help the Eco-security teams to monitor others. The Eco-security teams check who enters and leaves the Eco-city to stop unwelcome visitors from disturbing the peace of the Eco-society. They can investigate any wrongdoing of those who live and work in the Eco-city. The security teams will have adequate powers to remove offenders and hand them to the right authorities whenever necessary.

The responsibilities of Eco-security include the Eco-ICT-security teams continuously watching each other and investigating any security loopholes to eliminate possible cracking, hacking or cyberattack threats from destroying the Eco-city's IT systems.

The Eco-security teams will also work with the industries, businesses and Eco-research-and-innovation-centre to prevent any industrial espionage. And, because there are no prisons in the Eco-city, one of the other responsibilities is to have a presence in the rehabilitation centre to discipline, watch and control offenders under treatment.

If people have nothing to hide, they should allow trusted security personnel to monitor their activities to ensure their transparency and accountability. But if the security officers abuse their knowledge, then they will be prosecuted as well, because no one is immune or unaccountable for his or her actions.

The list of responsibilities may go on longer and it is up to the Eco-justice and Eco-security officers to define them and set up appropriate teams for the various protection functions.

BOOK TWO

UTOPIAN ECO-CITY

Dedication
to Book Two

Henri Maalouf declares:

If the poor become rich, the rich get richer.

When everyone on this planet can live self-sufficiently in an Eco-home, enjoying a decent standard of living, then humanity becomes morally advanced, evolves and ascends to a higher plane of existence. As I look at our civilisation, I see poverty and undignified living standards for 70 % of the human race and this means only 30% are civilised.

Therefore, I dedicate this book to all those who dream to own an Eco-home and make a plea to the leaders of the world to make such dreams come true. Maybe I am dreaming of a utopian planet that is so civilised it is like an advanced alien race living on another planet in outer space. There is nothing impossible if we have the relentless will to pursue our dreams. Building Eco-cities as described in this book is the first step towards providing Eco-homes to everyone on the planet.

The richest of this planet have enough wealth to build an Eco-home for each family using the excess money of the 63 wealthiest elite in the world. If peace dominates the earth and countries stop spending $1.6 trillion on weapons, they can build an Eco-home for each family. If corruption ends, governments can divert the wealth to the poor. If spending is prioritised to building homes, every family could have one. If systems are more efficient instead of being bureaucratic and micromanaging to control us more, the welfare systems can build more homes for the poor.

However, if investing in people includes everyone, productivity increases along with the national wealth. If personal, narcissistic greed ends and caring and sharing prevail, then more people will be lifted out of poverty. If people, elect those who build homes for them and make their lives better, people become wiser. If people fight for their rights to live free and dignified, they improve their lives. There are many ifs and buts; I hope there will be equality, justice and fairness for all.

I hope we can plant the seeds for more fruitful trees on our planet and remove the thorns from our bushes. It should be a compulsory human right to secure for each family an Eco-home in which to live an Eco-lifestyle as a safety net that eliminates poverty. Each family should be provided with universal credit to survive on the bare necessities and each capable person should work harder to enjoy more luxuries.

The Preamble to the Eco-City

In my Ecolism series of books, there are unfamiliar words such as Ecolism, Ecolist, Ecocracy and many nouns hyphenated with the prefix 'Eco-'. All of them mean more ethical, environmentally friendly or fairer systems to change human practices.

Ecolism is a new philosophy based on ethical principles for a new Eco-socio-economic system and Eco-friendly environment. The Eco-socio-economic system is a new social and economic system that follows the Ecolism's Eco-principles. The aim is to ensure self-sufficiency, sustainability, a greener environment and an end to poverty to create a peaceful, compassionate society living in a sustainable ecosystem.

Ecocracy is a new name given to the new Eco-socio-economic system as an alternative to democracy and other social and economic systems.

An *Ecolist* is a person who follows the Ecolism principles and lives an Eco-lifestyle in an Eco-society in any country.

Eco-principles are the directions for all laws and rules on the planet. The books in the Ecolism series are revolutionary guidelines for changing everything people do to become more ethical. The essence of the Eco-principles is responsible freedom, equality, justice, fairer-minded government policies and caring and sharing. In a nutshell, it is a cleaner living environment, fairer justice and better human rights for everyone on the planet.

Eco means environmentally friendly, but the concept of

Ecolism means much more. It changes everything humans do to more moral and ethical practices, recyclable and reusable consumables and a more-sustainable human ecosystem forever.

Introduction to the Eco-City

I have researched some topics in more depth than others for two reasons: the first is my lack of speciality in each one and the second is to make it easier to read without having too many details. However, depending on finances, available land and governments' will, the details can be worked out following the guidelines of the concept.

The Ecolism books aim to create more public awareness about the alternatives for building cities and houses the traditional ways. The concept of developing a new Eco-city is that instead of keeping adding to and modifying the existing ones without solving all the problems, we build a new one that does not have such issues. It is like an old car that keeps falling to pieces; we are better off buying a new one that remains intact.

I like my readers to take part in discussions and forums on my website (myecocity.co.uk) and to volunteer their ideas or expertise to help to create the most self-sufficient and economic Eco-city, surrounded by Eco-industries and large enough to employ and cater for all its residents.

The architectural design of the Eco-city is outside my specialisation when it comes to the details. However, it is a vivid dream I have seen since childhood about a city surrounded by a river. I did not know the details then, nor did I know about the meaning of 'Eco' or environmentally friendly. There was hardly any pollution worth mentioning 50 years ago. There were no plastic bags, packaging or plastic bottles. There were many fewer cars and people relied more on public transport. Also, there was a smaller amount of people on the planet and the required food supply was also smaller.

The cycle of life is birth and death recycled into different forms and different forms need different environments. Therefore, we must recycle our old, polluted cities into new ones and adapt them to produce 0% pollution and eliminate homelessness and poverty.

Summary of the Eco-City

Henri Maalouf declares:

If a city is full of sins and hard to purify, recycle it into a new one that is built to be pure and sin-free.
If we cannot make our socio-economic system fair for everyone, why don't we create a new, fairer one?

This summary is for those who do not have the time to read the detail of this book and want to know about the concept in brief.

The concept is to create one million Eco-homes in a self-sufficient and sustainable Eco-city, with surrounding Eco-industries and businesses. The aim is to employ all the unemployed, retired and anyone who can work for at least a few hours a day or a week. By doing so, governments can reduce the welfare spending and balance its economy. Consequently, more families can own Eco-homes, pay the mortgage, spend less and live better in an Eco-lifestyle.

The design of the Eco-city, accompanied by an Eco-socio-economic system as described in *Ecolism 1*, ensures a better standard of living for the poorest, reduces the amount of public money spent on the welfare system and saves billions. Consequently, the national productivity increases, the government debts decrease and growth and revenue balance the national deficits.

The Eco-city should have at least one million Eco-homes,

surrounded by Eco-businesses, Eco-agriculture and Eco-industries to employ its residents as long as they are capable of working. The design of the Eco-socio-economic system for living an Eco-lifestyle in an Eco-city is a self-sufficient, independent human ecosystem that interacts with others but protects itself first.

As an example, imagine if the European Union (EU), Scotland and Ireland shut their borders to England, would the English survive? There would be chaos, as there was in World War II. Therefore, the country's economic ecosystem must be self-sufficient to survive external influences or international economic turmoil. Perhaps, in such circumstances, farmers will learn to produce more and be competitive and people must buy local products, even if it is more expensive, to sustain the country's ecosystem as a matter of national security.

Each Eco-home in the Eco-city is prefabricated from timber and costs £100,000. The interest rate is currently between 1.5 and 3%, so the cost of interest is about £125 to £250/month for a family of four or for a couple living together. It is 75% cheaper than the renting or social-housing costs, which saves governments such as the United Kingdom (UK) government billions in housing benefits.

On the one hand, if people are unemployed, the welfare system should pay the interest on a guaranteed government mortgage loan. On the other hand, if the government employs the jobless, it pays nothing and collects more taxes. Employment must include the retired, elderly and physically challenged, who can flexibly work few hours a day or a week to earn enough to either pay the interest or repay the mortgage.

Building an Eco-city of one million Eco-homes, which costs £100 billion plus another £20 billion to be spent on its infrastructure, is probably beyond most governments' comprehension or ambition. However, if we have the will, we find ways to achieve our goals. The following outlines ideas to finance the Eco-city:

1. Any government, national trust, royal family or rich person may donate or lease public land on which to build the Eco-city and its surrounding Eco-industries.

2. The government can guarantee to pay the interest on the mortgage loans for those who are on social benefits. It will be cheaper than paying for any rent or cost to accommodate them.

3. Financing the Eco-city is open to any investor, great or small, who accepts a 1.5 to 3% guaranteed return on their investment. It will be more than people can get on their savings in a bank.

4. Charities, housing associations, lotteries providing funding, industries and businesses can participate in helping people to buy an Eco-home in the Eco-city. Moreover, they may be able to find the people jobs to repay the help or loans received.

5. The residents should live within their means and have an Eco-lifestyle of less outgoings than they would spend in ordinary cities. They should accept training in new skills suitable for the available jobs, so they are able to pay the interest on their mortgage as a minimum or make repayments towards the outstanding mortgage. It is better to build up equity in a property that they can use when they get frail, old and cannot work anymore, to spend on better care.

6. The government spending cost per head should follow the residents to the Eco-city to be spent on its infrastructure.

7. The government should license the Eco-industries and Eco-businesses to operate in the Eco-city, only if they employ

the locals, provide flexible hours and train their staff in the required skills; otherwise, their licences should be removed.

8. Eco-industries and businesses will be encouraged to move to the Eco-city to benefit from lower overheads by employing cheaper workers, 24/7 availability and flexibility, having free electricity, having free or leased land and having ring-fenced net tax-free profits of 5% on investment.

9. Each Eco-home will have an edible garden for people to grow their food, which is to prevent starvation under any circumstances and to reduce their outgoings. Each Eco-home will produce more electricity than it consumes, from renewable sources, to supply the industries with free electricity.

10. Each person should have access to the internet to learn and work from home, which is to save on costs for education or gaining vocational training skills.

11. Building a large Eco-city of one million Eco-homes should not be contracted to profiteering developers. The Eco-home should be designed and prefabricated for self-build following step-by-step instructions.

12. A group of seven people, which can include the unemployed and volunteers, can build an Eco-home in seven days; from this, they can earn credit to own one. However, there will be some conditions for acceptance attached. For example, the person must accept training on required new skills to work and pay at least the interest on the mortgage; otherwise, they risk losing it all and having to leave the Eco-city.

The Eco-city will not only help the unemployed, young and elderly to own a house but will also revive the industries, businesses and agriculture and save billions on the social-welfare system.

If Eco-homes in Eco-cities become the norm of our civilisation, only then does the social-welfare system become fair-minded, morally civilised and ethical.

In the UK, the United States of America (USA) and Germany, the unemployment rate is below 4.5 % in the year 2018. In the EU it varies from 2.4 to 21% in Greece and in other countries it starts at 0.1% and goes up as high as 95% in Zimbabwe. However, if each nation builds Eco-cities, the unemployment rate becomes 0%. Poverty, homelessness, insecure living and crimes all disappear. Only then can our civilisation become moral, caring and sharing and give people their complete human rights to live in a dignified manner.

I would like to repeat what I said in *Ecolism 1*: imagine if the USA creates peace on earth and stops spending more than $700 billion each year on weapons of mass destruction. Moreover, if the North Atlantic Treaty Organization (NATO) stops wasting 2% of their gross domestic product (GDP) on weapons, followed by other countries like Russia, China, India, Pakistan North Korea and so on. The USA can build Eco-cities in each state and give an Eco-home to every low -income family. Every American will become richer from such projects, including the political parties. Similarly, there will be no poverty or unemployment and there will be more prosperity in Europe and the rest of the world. Only then can our humanity become more morally civilised and an advanced human race.

Governments spend billions on discovering other planets, neglecting the perfection of planet earth. I wish they would spend more billions to eliminate poverty, to educate people more and to explore much more galaxies.

PART 1

Utopian Eco-City

Henri Maalouf declares:

If our cities cannot be environmentally and socially ideal for everyone, then should we not create new ideal Eco-cities?

The concept is to create one million Eco-homes in a self-sufficient, sustainable Eco-city, with surrounding Eco-industries to employ the locals and help them to pay the mortgages on their Eco-homes.

For example, each Eco-home in the UK could cost £100,000 and the interest is a maximum of £250/month for a couple or a family, which is much less than the rent or housing benefits paid to the unemployed in the UK. European countries have different welfare systems to support the unemployed and retired. But, as a minimum, they provide about £600/month and it is a burden on governments' budgets. But, if governments succeed to employ everyone, then that burden goes away.

Note: Other countries have different costs of living and different lifestyles. It varies from large populous nations, such as China, India, the USA and large countries in the EU, to small countries, such as Monaco and many small islands. Nevertheless, the principles remain the same: building Eco-homes to live self-sufficiently, spending less and living better. Of course, nothing can be free; people have to work to earn enough to pay the interest on the loan for an Eco-home as a minimum. Obviously, they have to work more to receive more and repay the cost of their shelter. If all fails, it is the governments' responsibilities to enhance the living standards of their people.

Any government can donate or lease public land for an Eco-city and its surrounding Eco-industries and guarantee the mortgage loans' interest for the unemployed. Therefore, financing the Eco-city is not a problem if it is open to any investor at a guaranteed maximum interest rate of 3%. The residents will live within their means in an Eco-lifestyle and must work at any job in the Eco-city to pay the interest or repay the mortgage. The Eco-socio-economic system, as described in *Ecolism 1*, is designed for the Ecolists to live on the lowest possible outgoings so they can accept lower hourly rates to become competitive and get a job.

Eco-industries and Eco-businesses will be encouraged to move to the Eco-city, as they would benefit from low overheads by employing cheaper workers, having free electricity, being granted land and having ring-fenced net profits of 5% on an investment. They will be very competitive, selling to the Eco-city, meeting its needs and exporting the excess at globally competitive prices.

Each Eco-home will have an edible garden for people to grow their food, so that nobody starves under any circumstances or in a national economic meltdown. Each Eco-home will produce more electricity than it consumes and should have an internet facility for people to learn and work from home through access to the rest of the world.

The Eco-councillors governing the Eco-city must be subject-matter experts in their departments and not politicians; they must share governance with committees from businesses and public representatives to cooperate and ensure the Eco-city's sustainability and self-sufficiency.

The new concept of the Eco-city is a complete human ecosystem with a socio-economic system where residents live an Eco-lifestyle governed by a new Eco-Magna-Carta as a new social charter of ethical principles, as described in *Ecolism 1*.

Building a paradisiacal Eco-city must be done in the most cost-effective ways, utilising every available space on the land for producing something useful, but without causing emissions of carbon dioxide (CO_2), nitrous oxide (N_2O) or any other harmful gases, using renewable energy sources, growing organic food and being surrounded by Eco-industries, Eco-businesses and Eco-agriculture.

Before we design an Eco-city, we must find the right land with sound geological conditions, positioned in a strategic location close to a major city with easy access to a seaport and airport. Undoubtedly, it should not be next to a volcano, as the Eco-city could be destroyed by its eruption; nor close to the sea, where it could be flooded by a tsunami (a giant sea wave); nor near earthquake zones with high seismic activity, nor in an area where it is vulnerable to a river flooding or any other disastrous force majeure possibility.

Once we find the right land, then we can design it to accommodate one million houses surrounded by a human-made river, a fence, sustenance zones and Eco-infrastructure, as suggested in the following sections.

However, before we start building an Eco-city, we must have a vision for an Eco-socio-economic system and Eco-lifestyle to ensure its success, self-sufficiency and sustainability.

The logic behind the Eco-solution is to save the inefficient spending of billions in our economy, to reduce the N_2O and

CO_2 emissions to 0% in an Eco-city, end unemployment and poverty and develop a new Eco-socio-economic system based on sustainability and self-sufficiency, which is fairer than capitalism, free of democracy's flaws and more successful than socialism.

The concept of the Eco-solution and its infrastructure is for people to work flexible hours according to their abilities and give better care to the elderly and society, from the cradle to the grave.

The new Eco-socio-economic system raises the living standards of the poor, gives the financiers reasonable profits and protects the interests of both, for a harmonious and sustainable coexistence. If everybody is reasonably happy and has a piece of the big cake, no one should fight to have more; equality and justice will then prevail.

In the Eco-city and under the new Eco-Magna-Carta of its Eco-socio-economic system, the governors, investors and workforce collaborate in a joint venture for long-term sustainability and the welfare of all. They work together like a chain that is as strong as its weakest link and where links must be removed or strengthened to maintain the total strength.

Humanity is still in a chaotic state, evolving randomly at various speeds in all directions and must have a better vision, better leadership and be on the right track for its train to reach a better destination.

Some people are still riding a slow train, which stops at many stations and is going in the wrong direction, while others are riding a super-fast one that never stops till it reaches its destination.

It is almost impossible to help every human to evolve at the same speed as others and reach the same level of enlightenment. Humans are not standard robots running the same program. They were created in various imperfect images, trying to evolve more and achieve perfection at multiple speeds.

Figure 1 Fast Train to Shanghai[1]

Figure 2 Slow Train to Katowice[2]

Some ride the fastest train for free, others cannot pay the fee for the slowest

However, I still believe that Eco-cities for similar groups of people will create more harmony, unity and alignment for them to follow the same path towards faster human evolution. Hence, it is unavoidable that there will be various types of Eco-cities in the world.

Therefore, the new Eco-socio-economic system leaves the current systems as they are, but offers an opportunity to those who would hop onto a different train going to an Eco-destination towards a more advanced social and utopian human ecosystem.

PART 2
The Benefits of the Eco-City

Henri Maalouf declares:

Solving a major problem needs a comprehensive solution;
addressing part of it creates loopholes for other ones.

The Eco-city solution will save billions on the social-welfare systems or taxpayers' money in Europe, the USA and other countries. It will revive the economy, reduce unemployment to near 0% and end poverty and homelessness. It will raise the minimum living standards and lower the cost of living simultaneously. People will live better and spend less. Furthermore, the new Eco-socio-economic system with the new Eco-lifestyle will direct people to live within their means in a fairer, freer society of equality and responsible Eco-freedom that works for everyone.

The Eco-city solution will also create new Eco-opportunities for businesses, industries and agriculture, to make the poor rich and the rich richer. Hence, the solution works for the rich as well as for the poor and the government, as long as each compromises a little bit.

For the Eco-solution to work in the USA, EU, UK or other countries, it is best if it is a sizeable Eco-city of one million houses, each having an edible garden and where the Eco-city has Eco-agriculture, Eco-businesses and Eco-industrial-zones.

It is vital that the Eco-city be large enough to find jobs for the various skills of its inhabitants.

Small countries might create an Eco-city or two, while a great big country like the USA might build an Eco-city in each of the 50 states. Hopefully, the EU would build at least one Eco-city in each of their member states.

One of the aims of the Eco-socio-economic system described in *Ecolism 1* is to save a high percentage of the public spending on the unemployed, pensioners and disabled. As an added value, employing them would convert them to taxpayers, instead of being a burden on the national welfare system.

To create a more competitive economic system, governments in Western countries must reduce the cost of living so people can accept lower wages to get a permanent job or work a few flexible hours to match their abilities. It is contrary to the ongoing trend of increasing the cost of living and having to raise wages with it, which increases unemployment and drives companies to invest in cheaper labour from other countries.

The proposed Eco-concept may look simple, but behind the concept is a sophisticated design. The challenge is to create a new Eco-socio-economic system that does not conflict with national laws and, at the same time, reduces peoples' outgoings.

When spending less to live, they can accept lower hourly rates to compete with cheaper labour from other countries and it encourages businesses to employ good-value-for-money and high-quality local workers with higher productivity.

The fundamental concept behind the Eco-solution is to build affordable, prefabricated Eco-homes from natural timber that will last for over 500 years and reduce the carbon footprint that results from other industrial materials used to create a house.

Buying an Eco-home must be accessible and affordable by any citizen, without them paying a deposit or subjecting them to credit scoring, a high-interest rate and other affordability checks. The condition for lending is that the government or the welfare system pays the interest on a mortgage, instead of rent and finds a job for the unemployed so they can pay the loan back.

The interest on a £100,000, three-bedroomed Eco-home is affordable by someone from even the most impoverished country in Europe or any deprived area in the USA. In a well-organised, self-sufficient and sustainable Eco-city, designed to help the residents grow their food and live on minimum expenditure, the Eco-socio-economic system of the Eco-city will not only save billions in government spending but will also enable the poor to survive any global economic recession, such as what happened in 2008 and the two world wars. Even if an Eco-city was isolated, people would not go hungry or be subjected to a dictatorial imperial power like the EU, such as what happened when the Greeks rebelled against the EU system and the Germans/EU shut down their banks.

The Eco-lifestyle in the Eco-city will reduce or diminish the costs of utility bills, transport, hospitals, schools, universities, security, insurances, bureaucracies, legal or professional fees and other areas of public spending to enable people to become more competitive and get a job or become self-employed and have recurrent revenue.

My logic for an economic Eco-lifestyle in an Eco-city is contrary to the inflationary trend of more expensive lifestyles and outgoings, which make unions ask for wage increases to cope with the cost of a higher living standard.

The trend of change is heading towards a rising cost of living and that is what makes Western countries less competitive. Companies keep influencing governments to allow them to recruit cheaper labour from other nations who accept lower wages and live a less-extravagant lifestyle. It is one of the main reasons why locals become redundant and become a burden on the taxpayers' contributions.

Therefore, politicians must create an environment for societies to live within their means, spend less and to accept less to become more competitive with other nations, but also have a reasonable standard of living.

A successful business person uses all the available money and resources wisely for higher profits. A government should do the same, invest in people and use everybody's potential to become more productive and efficient. Governments should learn from the Germans, South Koreans, Japanese and other successful nationalities.

The Eco-city has the potential to become an industrial Eco-city and a business centre to generate wealth equivalent to a commercial city like London or an industrial city like Munich, because it will be 100% productive, competitive and work will always be available for the locals at any age, working flexible hours to match their abilities.

One benefit of the Eco-socio-economic system is to save a high percentage of public spending on the unemployed, pensioners and disabled. The best way to achieve this is to reduce outgoings, pay lower wages to increase competitiveness, balance the cost of living with net income and create a system of flexible working hours available 24/7.

The proposed Eco-model may look simple, but behind it is a sophisticated design for how an Eco-society can live better, spend less, accept lower hourly rates to compete and live in a more self-sufficient, sustainable ecosystem.

Imagine how many billions the government can save by resolving the socio-economic problems for the poorest and most unproductive. The benefits of building a large Eco-city are much more than politicians envisage.

An Eco-lifestyle in an Eco-city will save on hospitals, schools, universities, security, insurances, bureaucracies, the legal system and other areas of public spending, to enable people to become more competitive and get a job or become self-employed and have more sustainable revenue.

An Eco-lifestyle supports the logic that says when people are wealthy they can afford luxuries, but when a person is underprivileged, will have no choice but to compromise and live on the necessities for survival. However, when even the basic needs for survival are not available, then more poverty, misery, crime and injustices emerge. Therefore, it is vital that we get the balance right, live an Eco-lifestyle, accept lower wages, spend less and work more.

The Eco-city will not only help the unemployed, young and elderly to own a house, but will also revive industry, businesses and agriculture. The politicians in the UK, USA and other countries, throughout a succession of governments, have converted capital cities into prosperous commercial cities, but have also destroyed the nation's industrial capabilities. This project may initiate a significant shake-up to create a new Eco-industrial-revolution to compete with the rest of the world.

Employing two million people to build an Eco-city and the Eco-industries that will manufacture what it needs and sell the excess is not that difficult, especially in an organised Eco-socio-economic system, where people have a lower cost of living and can afford to be competitive and accept lower hourly rates to get a job.

The industries will have the incentive to move to an Eco-city that provides competitive, high-quality, skilled workers at a lower cost, with free land and electricity, which reduces their overheads so that they may become more competitive and prosperous.

PART 3

The Eco-City's Success

Henri Maalouf declares:

The measure of a country's success is in its higher living standard, productivity and efficiency.

The success of building an Eco-city depends on meeting its objectives and pre-set criteria as proposed in the later sections.

However, the primary driver for building an Eco-city is the high demand for housing and the affordability of owning a house. Therefore, developing an Eco-city should not be another project for a developer to make massive profits from building it, so that it becomes expensive and unaffordable for the poor. Instead, it should be a great national project created by volunteers at the lowest cost possible.

The primary criterion to determine if this Eco-solution is successful is if the central government or a local authority donates or leases a sizeable area of public land, which is large enough to build one million three-bedroomed, detached Eco-homes with edible gardens, in an Eco-city surrounded by Eco-industries, business centres and agriculture.

The second most important criterion is whether the mortgage loans for the unemployed are guaranteed at a maximum rate of 3% fixed interest and 0% deposit, without a credit score requirement or any other unaffordable payment conditions.

The third most important criterion is whether the Eco-city's administration organises an Eco-lifestyle for the Eco-city's inhabitants, where no one can go hungry or live without shelter and provides social care and jobs at competitive rates for people to work and pay back the mortgage loan.

The fourth most important criterion is whether the Eco-social-economic system is put in place, forming a government troika of committees, consisting of specialist Eco-councillors, businesses and the workforce. A governing troika or tripartite system should always agree on the conditions and rules for the mutual benefits of everyone, ensuring continued sustainability and high productivity.

The fifth essential criterion is creating an Eco-bank capable of managing more than £100 billion for building the Eco-city and an Eco-commercial-bank managing more than £100 billion in investments for the industries.

The sixth criterion is building a large Eco-city of one million houses without contracting with traditional, expensive construction developers, but allows self-building for the unemployed in groups. The Eco-homes are a standardised prefabricated design and come with step-by-step instructions, to allow each of them to be built in seven days by seven people, supervised by professionals to make it easy for the non-professionals to build them.

The seventh criterion is that groups of volunteers can build their homes for virtual credit that can be paid as a deposit on a house.

The London 2012 Olympics' success was down to the 70,000 volunteers organising it. Imagine two million unemployed building the Eco-city of one million Eco-homes! Completing the

Eco-city may only take one year, providing that small carpentry factories are built for manufacturing the prefabricated building materials.

However, unlike the volunteers for the Olympics, who did not work for any reward, the builders of the Eco-city will get virtual credits for their working hours to use as a deposit for buying an Eco-home.

Moreover, the Eco-solution should not be a partisan project nor a commercial one. It should be a social motivation to build something great, like the Egyptians building the pyramids, but, instead, in our modern day and age, building a unique Eco-city and new Eco-socio-economic system.

PART 4

Financing the Eco-City

Henri Maalouf declares:

We are all equal before God, but if money is God, we are not!

There are about 7.7 billion human beings on our planet. Moreover, the total wealth is rising to about $280 trillion. The wealthiest 1% own 48% more than the most impoverished population. In other words, the 77 million richest people have more money than 3.7 billion of the poorest combined. According to Oxfam, 42 business people hold as much wealth as the 3.7 billion of the poorest. There are also wealthy pop stars, kings, princes, prime ministers and presidents of countries, most of whom hide their actual wealth in hedge funds and secretive offshore accounts.

There is more than $33 trillion hidden in trusts and secret offshore tax-haven accounts in Switzerland, Germany, Luxembourg, the USA, Singapore, the Cayman Islands, the Virgin Islands and many other small countries. But who knows the truth? They are secretive funds for businesses and bribed politicians. Also, the global derivatives market is worth $1.2 quadrillion while the total GDP of all countries is rising to £100 trillion.

Such wealth in the world poses these questions: *Why does poverty still exist? Why is there a wide gap between the wealthy* *and the poor? Why do the elite few have much more than they ever need, while the poor are desperate for food? Why do nearly half of the population of the planet or more than 3.6 billion people live on less than $2/day?*

I am not suggesting communism or socialism as a solution, but I am not defending capitalism either. The Eco-socio-economic system is a concept to protect the fundamental human rights and ensure a decent standard of living for the poorest as a minimum. There are enough pieces of the big cake to go around for everyone on this planet. Some have bigger bellies than others, some can eat but have no food, others have more food than they can chew.

There are adequate funds on this planet to build a series of Eco-cities of all sizes, shapes and forms to remove poverty from every country. However, the current trend in any housing project ends up with more money for developers and suppliers that makes a house unaffordable by the poor. Notably, there are strict conditions that cannot be met by the unemployed and those who are on a low income. Hence, they cannot own a house. Additionally, the retired, those blacklisted by credit-scoring agencies and those unable to get a deposit have no hope of climbing the housing ladder.

The Eco-socio-economic system allows even the homeless to own a house, have an address to become entitled to housing benefits and benefits from the welfare system. Note: In the UK, if people do not have an address, they cannot benefit from the welfare system and the government does not automatically house them to give them an address! Hence, they become homeless and street beggars to survive. I am sure there are similarities even in most Western countries.

The formula is simple: an affordable Eco-home costs £100,000 and, based on 1.5 to 3% interest, it would cost between

£125 to £250/month for a family of four to live in an Eco-home. It is affordable for any working family in most countries and is even much less than any monthly rent or housing benefits paid by Western governments for the unemployed or retired. On average, renting in the UK costs about £1,000/month when paid by the welfare system, while paying interest on a £100,000 Eco-home is less than £250/month. Governments are short-sighted if they do not invest in social housing and save billions.

The cost of the estimated infrastructure for an Eco-city is about £40 billion plus. The government could finance it by diverting the funds from some needless projects to the Eco-city or redirecting the public spending per head for the two to four million people who will move to the Eco-city. Therefore, the public expenditure per head follows them and so there is no need for extra government borrowing or spending for such a priority project.

Finances for the Eco-city could come from various sources, such as local and global private lenders, banks, industries and businesses, provided that the investments are guaranteed by the government. Of course, it is up to the investors to accept lower interest and a lesser amount of profits depending on global competition, turnover and interest rates at the time of borrowing, which varies in different countries.

When investment is open to everybody, then anyone could invest any amount of money. Investors can choose to lend, either for an Eco-home at a guaranteed 3% profit maximum or invest in any business or industry that guarantees 5% tax-free minimum profits. This way some people can get more revenue on their savings than what they get from keeping it in a bank.

The Eco-taxation system will allow 5% tax-free profit to encourage investors to move to the Eco-city, train and hire locals, pay taxes from revenues gained above the 5% tax-free threshold allowed and enjoy lower overheads and the Eco-city's free facilities.

There is a high percentage of struggling elderly with lots of equity in their houses that exceeds £100,000, who could easily downgrade to have spare cash to look after their health better and enjoy a more comfortable life in their retirement. The charities that take care of the elderly and disabled could also help to support them when living in an Eco-home in an Eco-city.

Housing associations could get a better return on their investment from buying Eco-homes in the Eco-city and anybody with access to loans or equity could do the same. Therefore, financing the Eco-city will not be a problem and could be done without creating a burden on the national budget.

Nevertheless, one can envisage more open inward investment opportunities from the rest of the world, including private investors, governments, all the global banks and anybody with enough money to invest in an Eco-home for £100,000 to benefit from 3% interest. The flow of investment will be overwhelming. Even industries can invest in their factories and build Eco-homes for their employees to guarantee their loyalty for many years to come.

Even the worst government could see the economic sense in prioritising the Eco-city project as the best investment and value for taxpayers' money. Governments spend billions on the welfare system and social issues for the unemployed, getting nothing in return. However, if the taxpayers' money were spent to build the Eco-city and employ the unemployed, it would be paid back through the profits from the tax revenues.

Furthermore, governments do need to invest billions, but must guarantee the loans and probably need to spend £20 billion to £40 billion on the Eco-city's infrastructure instead of spending on less important projects. The benefits of building an Eco-city to serve two to four million citizens outweighs the benefits of any other national projects, such as high-speed rail or even a nuclear power plant or increasing international aid, while poverty and homelessness exist at home.

PART 5
Eco-Cities of the World

In ancient history, the Greek philosopher Plato, in 423 BC, raised his philosophical teachings about the flaws in socio-economic systems. He discussed, in his book *The Republic*, capitalism, tyranny and democracy. He came up with a solution called timocracy. It means *the love of honour is the motive for rules*; in other words, the ethical should rule. Does it exist nowadays?

Ethics in politics and business practices hardly exist around the world in the 21st century and yet we give ourselves the title 'civilised'. In my opinion, humanity has a long way to go yet to deserve such a title. However, of course, some are morally more civilised than others and the percentage is decreasing by the day.

The richest or lobbyists are the real rulers, influencing politicians to legislate what is better for their vested interests and higher profits at any cost and not necessarily what is ethical, ideological or better for the wellbeing of the humankind.

The Eco-concept is a modern version of timocracy. I call it Ecolism or you could call it Ecocracy. It is a tripartite-governance Eco-socio-economic system formed from an efficient workforce, moral rulers and ethical investors. They have to keep the balance of an ecosystem to maintain its sustainability and protect it by making it self-sufficient in all its requirements.

Note: Eco-self-sufficiency does not mean agriculture and food only. It means the ability to work and self-pay for education, health, home and other expenditures required for a decent living standard. Therefore, it is essential that the socio-economic system and Eco-lifestyle are created, preferably in a large Eco-city, to supplement the individual ability to live self-sufficiently. The Eco-socio-economic system is designed to provide those necessities at a much cheaper cost to enable people to become competitive in work and pay for the cost of dignified living.

In the recent history of the UK, Sir Ebenezer Howard, in 1898, created the garden-city concept, which was intended to develop well-planned, self-contained communities surrounded by a greenbelt, holding proportionate areas of residence, industry and agriculture. However, unfortunately, the concept has changed to a more commercial project rather than being a rational and social design.

Since then, the idea has spread around the world and many small projects have taken place. Eco-cities of one kind or another have been built in Latin and North America, South Africa, Europe and Australia and there is the Kibbutz in Israel set up in 1909. Recently, Abu Dhabi has created the Masdar Eco-city, China is still building Chinese Eco-cities and cooperating with Tianjin Eco-city in Singapore and, in India, the small Auroville Eco-city is being constructed by local people, while in 2015 the Indian government launched a national initiative to build smart cities.

Most of the above Eco-cities are comparatively small projects for small populations and none have an internal, devolved, local government based on the new ethical Eco-socio-economic system. Most Eco-cities in the world concentrate on solar energy and an Eco-environment, touching on local employment, good health and transport, but has no social charter for a harmonised, ethical and peaceful community living in an Eco-socio-economic system such as that described in *Ecolism 1*.

Therefore, these Eco-city projects have environmental and commercial aspects, but they are missing the social Eco-lifestyle and their suitability for the poorest to live a cost-effective lifestyle. In my concept, the Eco-city should not be luxurious and must be economical in all of its aspects and built for sustainable self-sufficiency that is unaffected by national or global economic turmoil or external influences.

The infrastructure layout in the following chapter outlines the proposed Eco-city design for Western countries. However, other nations might adapt the model to suit their geography, economy and culture.

.

PART 6
The Eco-City's Infrastructure

The Eco-city has three primary sectors encircling each other, starting from the outermost perimeter surrounding the Eco-sustenance sector, followed by the Eco-city's residence sector in the middle and the central section of the Eco-city's council.

The visionary Eco-city's layout is like the circles of a lake rippling out to navigate from the centre to the edges. It has a symmetrical design with smaller to greater circles and sections accessed by three sets of ten gates for each sector. It features Eco-gates, Eco-rivers, Eco-fences, Eco-industries, Eco-businesses, Eco-agriculture and Eco-homes. Note: The Eco-home design will be detailed in *Ecolism 4*.

It is not like any other Eco-city created throughout history; it has a new Eco-socio-economic system for shared governance between the councillors/administrators, businesses and residents. As repeatedly mentioned in the Ecolism books, the principal design components are sustainability, self-sufficiency, environmental friendliness and providing an economical Eco-lifestyle, where the Eco-society lives in harmony and peace, with the fundamental human rights being for each couple to own an Eco-home, work and pay for it.

Eco-City Perimeters

The Eco-city's perimeters are made of three concentric rings to surround the three sectors. Each circular boundary has a fence, ten gates and a river running inside it, followed by a ring road that connects to the main crossroads through many roundabouts (traffic circles through which to access the streets for the houses and to travel across the three sectors).

Eco-Fences

The Eco-city protects itself from unwelcome intruders and surrounds its perimeters with barriers of conifer trees and bushes, walls, rivers, cameras, motion detectors and so forth. Alongside each fence, there are gates to accept or reject visitors. Although monitoring technologies do not need walls and can detect what is behind them, it is a bonus to have a reliable and physical separation as well. The security guards can use any technology that triggers alarms to alert them about a threat, which is currently available in most countries to protect their borders.

The Eco-fences have sensors to detect anyone digging tunnels under them. Also, some ultrasonic and electromagnetic pest-repelling devices can be installed to drive away rodents, insects and other vermin. There are unique trees that absorb and may prevent airborne viruses or any technology that can prevent or burn viruses would be a good thing to implement.

The First Eco-Fence

The first Eco-fence is the outer border of the Eco-city, surrounding its sustenance zones to prevent intruders and control the access of eligible visitors via its gates.

The shape of the first perimeter fence will depend on the available land. The ten gates should be at an equal distance from each other and at each corner of its irregular decagon shape. Primarily, the fence should be good enough to protect the industries and facilities of the Eco-city. It should allow controlled access to the businesses, agriculture, industries and other services of the Eco-sustenance sectors without accessing the Eco-city's residence area, which is surrounded by another perimeter and gates.

The Second Eco-Fence

The second Eco-fence separates the Eco-city's residence sector from the Eco-sustenance sector. It also has ten gates at each corner of its regular-shaped decagon. The primary purpose of the gates is to give easy access to its residents and the Eco-sustenance sectors, also to prevent unwelcome visitors or intruders.

The Third Eco-Fence

The third Eco-fence surrounds the Eco-council sector and has a similar layout to the Eco-city's residence sector, but smaller and its primary purpose is to protect, control and restrict the traffic to the Eco-council sector and the committees of representatives.

Eco-Gates

The first set of gates allows access to the Eco-sustenance sector from outside the Eco-city, the second to the Eco-city's residence sector in the middle and the third to the Eco-council sector at the centre.

Each gate is a checkpoint to verify identities and allow approved visitors into a sector. Moreover, the outer set of gates must have detectors for weapons, explosives, chemicals and forbidden materials.

Each gate has computer systems running a facial-recognition software application to scan each person entering the Eco-city and it connects to the national database to verify the identity of wanted criminals. The security personnel give a photo ID pass to each visitor and possibly a wrist tracking band to track the person's location. A specialist security team control the gates and have powers to investigate and vet anybody.

Eco-City-Rivers

The human-made Eco-city-rivers around the Eco-city have multipurpose functions. They are used for farming fish to feed the Ecolists and they collect rainwater that is pumped to the water-treatment plants and then distributed as needed.

The Eco-city's streets and roads have specially designed channels on their sides to collect the water and pour it into the nearest Eco-river's access point. Optionally, each Eco-river's bank might have a resting channel for settling the dirt and sand out of the water as an initial filtration phase, after which the water is pumped into the Eco-river.

The Eco-rivers must be kept hygienic and not polluted by

any fuel from boat engines, dirt or the forbidden plastic bags, which is to make it easier to filter, treat and distribute to the residential, agricultural, industrial and other areas, depending on the purity level needed.

The Eco-river must have specialist equipment to aerate and oxygenate the water for healthier fish. Water-fountain pumps can be installed to create beautiful fountains that aerate the water and have coloured lights to create beautiful scenes.

The Eco-city can also use systems to prevent ice from forming on the surface and cultivate aquatic plants for supplemental filtration. There are some types of water plants that absorb ammonium, nitrates and phosphates and help to assimilate other undesirable substances. This natural process improves the water quality while shading the river from light, especially if algae grows and covers all the surface.

The Eco-City-River-Banks

The outer side of the Eco-city's river bank that reaches the fence is a feeding ground for the livestock. The cattle produce milk and their meat feeds the Eco-city's residents; chickens and their eggs are also additional food. The animals will have housing structures to protect them from a harsh winter and to store their food supplies. The animals' shelter is attached to the fence to improve its security.

The other, inner, side of the river bank is for the light entertainment of the elderly and others. People may enjoy promenading, feeding the ducks and sitting in cafés, drinking tea and eating locally made healthy sweets. They can also socialise with each other and play stimulating mental games to improve their memory and minds.

The inner side of the river bank joins a promenade structured with lanes for cycling, pedestrians and scooters. The promenade encircles the outermost main ring road of the Eco-city's residence and has wind turbines, fruit trees and berry bushes that also act as a wall preventing vehicles from crashing into the boardwalk.

The Eco-City-River for the Sustenance Sector

The Eco-sustenance sector has a river that is smaller in width but longer. It runs inside the outer perimeter of the first Eco-fence and serves the Eco-sustenance areas. It also collects the rainwater from the sustenance area and stores it to supply the agricultural land and other zones. The river can have fish to feed the industrial workers and the river bank could also have cattle roaming free, grazing on the grass to save cutting it and allowing the residents to benefit from the cattle's meat and milk.

The Eco-City's Main River for Residents

The Eco-city's river inside the second fence is the widest one, proportionally designed for the Eco-city's size and population and its purpose is to serve the Eco-city's residents by providing water and fish supplies.

Also, it collects the rainwater from the Eco-city to store it and act as its reservoir. The Eco-city's river will also display beautiful scenes with the floating Eco-fountains and water-lily flowers and will be kept clean to produce drinking water for the Eco-city. The cattle roam free on its banks, as do birds and domesticated animals.

The Eco-City-River for the Centre

The Eco-council-sector river inside the third Eco-fence is a small, narrow stream that will help with the necessities of fish and water for the Eco-council and its administration buildings outside the fence.

Eco-Ring-Roads

Behind each fence and river is an Eco-ring-road surrounding each of the three sectors and the central administration. The outermost is the Eco-sustenance-ring-road, which encompasses the Eco-sustenance sections and is the longest. It connects to the main roads across the sustenance zones and the cross-sectional streets of the industries, businesses, agriculture and other services for the Eco-city.

The middle one is the Eco-residence-ring-road, which surrounds the residential areas and is the widest. It connects to the main roads across the Eco-city and its inner streets. It has the promenade on its outer side, as mentioned earlier.

The next innermost is the Eco-admin-ring-road, which surrounds the Eco-administration outside the Eco-council's fence and has parking spaces on both of its sides. It must be wide enough for all the Eco-administration visitors.

The fourth is the Eco-council-ring-road, inside the Eco-council's fence and it is the smallest and interconnects the streets leading to each Eco-council.

Eco-Main-Roads

This Eco-city has ten main crossroads, starting from the Eco-city's perimeter of the sustenance sections, crosses the second boundary surrounding the residence area and continues to the third perimeter of the administration centre. Outside the Eco-city's perimeter and opposite each of its ten gates, there are parking areas for vehicles. The Eco-city does not allow cars to enter for security reasons and fossil-fuel-powered cars cause pollution. The Eco-transport provides park and ride, electric transport buses for visitors and trucks or trailers for deliveries.

Each bus has a driver and an inspector to take photos of the passengers and transmits them to the gate for facial-recognition inspection to check if any person had a criminal record or is not allowed to enter certain sections of the Eco-city. It is done this way to save inspection time at the gate and reduce traffic congestion at the point of entry.

The traffic passes through any of the ten outer gates to a specific destination. Once the first checkpoint has authorised access, the drivers navigate the roundabouts that divert the electric vehicles to the desired destination. The drivers either access the Eco-sustenance section or continue to the gates of the Eco-city's residential area for another checkpoint.

Each of the ten main roads starts at each of the decagon's corners and cross to the opposite one. Each road has five lanes (car-width tracks) going into the Eco-city and five lanes to return. The vehicle tracks are marked for speeds of 100mph, 80mph, 60mph, 40mph and 20mph, consecutively.

The centre of the two-way road is one lane wide and covered by berry bushes, so that there is no wasted space and it helps to supply the Eco-city with the most nutritious and anti-oxidant berry fruits. Between the berry bushes, there are giant wind turbines to generate electricity for the Eco-city. The street lights are fixed on the posts of the wind turbines and activated by motion detectors to save on consuming electricity.

Each side of the main roads has a wide multifunction pavement. On the left-hand side of the pavement, there are also condensed berry bushes, fruit trees and designer wind turbines shaped like flowers, sculptures or trees that are pleasant to the eye. The berry bushes and fruit trees supply fruits and the designer wind turbines supply electricity.

The berry bushes between each side of the main roads and the pavements are necessary to function as a natural fence to safeguard the pedestrians and cyclists from any accidental car collisions or a car losing control in remaining on the road's lanes.

The multifunction pavement has a utilities tunnel for water, fibre-optic cable and electricity supplies, designed in a way that does not cause any interruption for the traffic or the pedestrians. Alongside it, there is one track for scooters, another for cyclists and the third one is for pedestrians. The right-hand side of the pavement joins the sides of the houses and ends at the beginning of each inner street. The crossings between the pavements and the inner streets are either underground or have pedestrian traffic lights.

Eco-Inner-Streets

The inner streets of the Eco-sustenance sections can be designed by the industries and businesses to suit their buildings and borders, crossing the ten main roads coming from outside the Eco-city.

The internal streets of the Eco-city's residence sector are between each row of Eco-homes that are back to back, separated by their gardens and facing one lane of the internal street that joins the main roads in both directions.

The inner streets also have pavements for pedestrians, cycles and scooters; utility tunnels; and water drainage that joins the ones in the main road going to the rivers. At each end of an internal street, where it meets the main road, there is a bus stop for taking passengers to the centre or the Eco-city's perimeter and also steps to the underground for the train stations.

The inner streets of the Eco-council sector conform with the general layout of the Eco-city and separate the Eco-councils from each other, but join them to the Eco-assembly-centre.

Eco-Transport

The Eco-transport system must use electric vehicles, as described later in the Eco-research-and-innovation section under the Eco-sustenance sector. The underground trains run under the main roads from the centre to the Eco-sustenance areas, for the residents to quickly arrive at work and return home, with less-frequent stops.

The buses and slow vehicles will run in the 40 and 20mph slow lanes, take passengers from the Eco-city residence area to the centre or its perimeter and sometimes to the train stops.

A bus transport service will be provided in the Eco-sustenance sections for people to get to their work from the train stops. The Eco-sustenance area's buses will only allow the Eco-city's employees, who have their IDs and personal Eco-card, to ride them between their place of work and train or bus stops.

The Eco-city will have autonomous Eco-cars for the Eco-councillors, businesses, some visitors and those who can afford them, for private transport. All electric Eco-vehicles (bicycles, tricycles, scooters and others.) can be used inside the Eco-city. Each Eco-vehicle will be tagged, tracked and not be allowed to leave the Eco-city. Therefore, there will be no need to lock it when parked at a location.

PART 7

The Eco-City's Sectors

As mentioned earlier in the Eco-infrastructure layout, the Eco-city has three sectors or divisions: Eco-sustenance, Eco-residence and the Eco-council with its central administration. In the following sections, there are more details about the infrastructure of each sector, starting from the centre, followed by the residence zone and ending in the Eco-sustenance zones.

The Eco-City's Council Sector

The Eco-city's centre naturally houses the Eco-council, businesses and public-representatives committees. The efficient Eco-socio-economic system's logic is to accommodate people closer to their work if working from home is not practical. Therefore, the Eco-councillors, representatives, specialist advisors and secretaries will live inside the Eco-city's centre and the Eco-homes are identical to the ones in the rest of the Eco-city to follow the Eco-equality principle.

The Eco-City's Administration Sector

The Eco-city's administration or civil services are an expansion of the Eco-council, is located outside the Eco-city-centre in the Eco-administration area and runs all its required functions. Its location and buildings are outside the Eco-council zone's fence, surrounded by the Eco-admin-ring-road. Each administration has its own building or part of it and can be expanded by building more floors or sharing with others.

The Eco-city's administration departments deal directly with the Ecolists for all their requirements, including education, health, employment and anything that is related to their wellbeing and welfare Consequently, the Eco-administration deals with agriculture, industries, businesses and other organisations.

The flow of people coming to the Eco-council or its administration will have scheduled appointments to meet somebody and will leave as soon as the meeting is over to reduce any congestion or queueing.

The Eco-city's system reduces congestion from people coming to the centre by minimising the need for physical meetings and replacing them with virtual ones using video-conferencing technology as much as possible, which records all conversations for transparency and accountability.

The Eco-city is open for business 24/7 and the flow of people can be spread out through shift work to reduce congestion and not suffer from congestion charges.

The Eco-city may customise a video-conferencing system, such as Skype for business or Web-ex or MS Lync to communicate with the residents. Each resident may own an Eco-mobile-phone, (aka an Eco-cell-phone in the USA) or an Eco-tablet that connects through a fast 5G Eco-bandwidth that runs on a specific frequency or the equivalent Eco-city's Wi-Fi connection to the Eco-data-centre, which enables any person to communicate at any time from any location.

The Eco-City's Residence Sector

The housing areas start inside the Eco-residence-ring-road of the Eco-city and end outside the Eco-admin-ring-road in the centre.

The first outer ring of the Eco-homes, around the residential area, should be specially designed bungalows suitable for the elderly and physically challenged to give them a more comfortable life. The main reason for choosing this location is to provide them with quicker access to the riverbank where they can walk to remain active and enjoy being with each other, doing things of common interest.

The second outer ring is for schools, universities, vocational centres, mini-hospitals or medical clinics, restaurants, cafés, leisure facilities and fitness centres. These facilities should be distributed equally across the ten sections of the Eco-city. Using the front-line services should be free or subsidised by the Eco-welfare system for the poor, unemployed and those not earning enough to afford them. The rest of the rings and segments will be the bulk of the private Eco-homes, reaching the outer side of the Eco-admin-ring-road.

The foundations of the Eco-homes should be durable enough for future expansion and provisioned to build another two floors on top of each Eco-home. Therefore, the infrastructure should be scalable enough to expand and accommodate the future population capacity.

The Eco-City's Sustenance Sector

The Eco-sustenance sector surrounds the Eco-city's residence area and consists of many segments intended to suit the space needed by each Eco-sustenance zone. Each business or service might occupy a physical space in the Eco-sustenance sector, but the zone covered by its services may include the entire Eco-city.

The industrial buildings might have a basement and two or more floors on top, initially and can expand horizontally or vertically to occupy more areas. The warehouse section, for example, might need a small segment, while the agriculture section might require more land outside the Eco-city. Hence, its zone includes the streets' trees and the Eco-homes' gardens. The Eco-city could build foundations for business buildings that are robust enough for more than 30 floors high and the businesses might construct their structures but retain the pre-planned virtual design of each shared building.

The energy and water plants might fit in one segment, but the entire Eco-city is the zone for each. The Eco-ICT-data-centre is in two parts, occupies two locations and supplies services to the whole Eco-city, its businesses and the world.

PART 8

Climate Change

Henry Maalouf declares:

Destroying our environment destroys us.

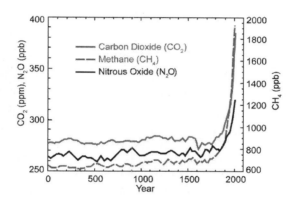

Figure 3 Climate change[3]
Note the sharp rise in ppb of CO_2, CH_4 and N_2O since the 20th century

You do not have to be a scientist to observe the effects of climate change. Just watch the number and intensity of heat waves across the world increasing year by year. Watch the oceans rising and taking more of the lands. Look at the glaciers melting faster than they should. Gaze at the droughts drying up the rivers and green lands.

I used to stare at the sun and enjoy getting a suntan for hours at the beach 50 years ago; now I feel like cancer starts to eat my skin after few minutes of exposing my body to the sun. What has humanity done to the ozone layer to weaken it and allow the sun's rays to cause damage to our planet? We have become like firefighters entering a fire without protective clothing. Eventually, the fire burns the firefighters alive.

The scientists might argue about the history of climate change, but 99% agree that the temperature has been sharply rising since 1950 due to human activities accelerating the production of greenhouse gases, which has increased the rise in global temperatures.

The largest producers of harmful gases are China, the USA and the EU, due to their industries and vehicles. They are destroying the planet slowly for profits, while there are other ways to maintain the ecosystems and make profits.

We do not have to be scientists to understand the graphs or observe the rise in sea levels, tides and the waves' height during extreme weather. Many countries worldwide are enhancing their seawall defences to stop high waves from hitting coastal habitation.

Globally, we see severe floods and droughts, the melting of the glaciers, tornadoes, tsunamis, a high ultraviolet (UV) index that can cause cancer and hotter summers because of climate change and the rise in temperature that has resulted from human activities polluting the earth, most notably since 1950.

The rise of CO_2 started when humans learned about agriculture and livestock, and then the industrial revolution exponentially increased pollution to the point of no return. Trillions of trees were cut without being replaced, billions of vehicles were manufactured using fossil fuels, billions of barrels of oil were produced and the list goes on regarding chemicals, plastics and others. Hence, you see in the graph above the sharp rise in CO_2, N_2O and HC_4.

Thinking logically, we can conclude that the 7.7 billion people on this planet are accelerating the production of the greenhouse gases contributing to the sharp rise in global temperatures, by merely inhaling oxygen and exhaling CO_2, not to mention what else they do to the environment.

The highest contributors are CO_2 and N_2O from burning fossil fuels for cars and industries. The other contributing factor to CO_2 production is from forestry and the misuse of wastelands. An additional contributor is the methane (CH_4) produced by the excessive numbers of livestock needed to feed the massive population on this planet.

The air we inhale naturally consists of 78% nitrogen, 20% oxygen, 0.04% carbon dioxide, other gases and pollutants. We inhale about 21% oxygen and exhale 16% of it. However, we inhale 0.04% carbon dioxide and exhale 4% of it to clean our blood. So, the 7.7 billion people on this planet are a CO_2 production factory.

The creation of Eco-cities and Eco-lifestyles are the beginning of reducing greenhouse gases from human activities. Every combustion engine must be replaced by an electric motor to stop us from using gas and petrol. Also, we must stop using aerosol sprays and volatile organic compounds (VOCs), which are chemicals and pollutants regularly used in most houses or some industries.

There are many natural sources of renewable energy that do not pollute our environment or upset the natural balance of the earth. However, positions are influenced by businesses who care about short-term profits at the expense of slowly destroying the planet's environment and effecting devastating climate change.

The following are some of the renewable energy sources that

are suitable for one million houses at a lesser cost than a nuclear power plant: downdraft energy towers, terrestrial solar-energy satellites, solar-energy plants, wind-turbine farms, geothermal energy, hydro energy, tidal lagoons and wave power. As we make technological and scientific progress, the future innovations will improve existing ones and compete with nuclear and fossil fuel.

In the Eco-city, all the Eco-homes, business premises, industrial buildings, agriculture lands and the roads should have highly efficient solar panels and wind turbines to generate electricity from renewable sources. Moreover, instead of feeding the power back to the grid, it is stored in new, advanced, molten-salt, thermal energy, giant storage tanks and batteries for use during the day or night.

The new advances in renewable-energy technologies are making it cheaper than nuclear power plants and fossil fuels, especially when it is in mass production and is locally manufactured. However, a power grid and generators as backups must be available for IT and the industries for continuous 24/7 availability.

PART 9

The Eco-Sustenance Zones

The Eco-city's sustenance zones are primarily to serve the Eco-city, but can also sell products and services to the rest of the world.

Initially, some industries, businesses and agriculture will have about four million people to serve. They are not well-off customers capable of spending a significant amount of money on luxuries, but their necessities are still substantial enough to kick-start the relevant industries or businesses and cover their overhead costs with the allowed tax-free profits of 5% to guarantee the return on their investments.

The Eco-city will equip the industries with almost free facilities and a good-value-for-money workforce available 24/7, which will reduce their overhead and help them to become more competitive in selling their products to the rest of the world.

The designs and types of the Eco-sustenance sectors will depend on the Eco-city's requirements; once these are met, businesses can sell outside the Eco-city. The Eco-industries and businesses will always follow the Eco-principles, code of conduct and ethics, especially abiding by the Eco-environment principle of 0% human-made pollution.

The main roads and streets in the Eco-sustenance areas should have wind turbines, fruit trees and berry bushes on their sides like the rest of the Eco-city. Also, each industry or type of agriculture should have a giant 9MW wind turbine with electricity storage to become electrically self-sufficient.

The business buildings should have motorised, sun-tracking solar panels on their roofs and wind turbines to generate electricity and store it in batteries.

The Eco-sustenance's sectors roads and streets must also have utility tunnels for the fibre-optic cables connected to the Eco-ICT-data-centres, electric wires, drains and other facilities. It should be at the side of its pavements for easy access and cause no disruption to the traffic or require the digging up of the road for maintenance.

The following chapters describe a concept design and facilities as guidelines to be adopted for the Eco-city.

The industries and businesses may design their own buildings, but must follow the Eco-city's principles and its Eco-socio-economic system to address the climate-change challenges, as discussed throughout the Ecolism books.

PART 10
The Eco-Energy Zone

Henri Maalouf declares:

If we protect our environment, nature will protect us.

The Eco-energy zone might need an entire segment in the Eco-sustenance area, but its zone will extend to any solar-, wind- and geothermal-energy installations in the Eco-city.

The Eco-city will produce its Eco-energy from renewable sources and there is no need for the excessive cost of nuclear power plants, coal, petrol products or shale gas.

The Eco-renewable-energy plants are the best way to reduce the human-made CO_2 and N_2O emissions to 0%. Building Eco-cities is the best solution for cutting the greenhouse-gas effect and moving people from their current polluted cities to cleaner ones is the best option. The revolutionary change in how we should build cities and convert them into Eco-environmental ones will clean up our planet and make us more civilised.

We should always recycle our waste and reuse our tools, carrier bags, utensils and all consumables to recycle our polluted industrial cities and transform them into cleaner Eco ones.

Energy Cost Comparison

The cost of energy varies among countries depending on which technology they use and from which power source it comes. It also ranges from one year to another as the technological advances progress. In China and Korea, it is a third of the cost of energy in the UK and the EU and in the USA, it is 25% cheaper than in the EU. Although oil and gas may compete with all other energy sources, it is very detrimental to the environment and continuously produces more CO_2 and N_2O than any other energy sources.

However, pretty soon, renewable energy will be cheaper than energy from fossil fuels, such as crude oil, coal and natural gas and nuclear energy. The oil producers know these facts and therefore they are trying to reduce petroleum prices to compete with the cheaper, renewable energy sources, but politicians always make things more expensive to please their lobbyists.

Let us take an example of building a nuclear power station in a few countries. The cost of building a nuclear power plant in the UK is about £90/MWh; the Chinese can construct it for £24/MWh and Norway will supply electricity in the year 2020 that will cost £18/MWh. In the USA, it is more expensive than in China and Korea, but it is 25% less than in the UK and the EU. The cost comparison for various sources of energy is very conflicting and depends on the technologies used, tax levies, capital costs and many other factors.

The electricity cost from nuclear sources is cheaper than gas and coal, but when the petroleum prices dropped it was no longer the case and, in time, renewable energy sources will be cheaper, safer and better for the planet; the others will be things of the past.

No matter what the economic argument presents, the trend

is going towards renewable energy sources that are free from harmful environmental pollution. Renewable energy from natural and cleaner sources avoid the risk of nuclear radiation and the prohibitive cost of investing in it. The excessive cost of getting rid of nuclear waste is neither economical nor environmentally friendly.

It is wiser and more civilised to pay a higher price for renewable energy to protect the environment and ensure the longer existence of this planet.

The renewable energy sources will become cheaper than nuclear energy if the latest technologies are implemented and mass produced and will have much lower overhead costs. It becomes more achievable when building one million Eco-homes for an Eco-city and everything is locally manufactured by cheaper workers.

In the Eco-city, we should create renewable-energy factories to employ thousands of the locals instead of paying the Chinese, Koreans or the French to build a nuclear power plant.

However, as the nuclear energy cost goes down if constructed by the Chinese and Koreans, the efficiency of solar photovoltaic cells and wind turbines is going up. So, the cost of renewable energy becomes lower than nuclear and fossil-fuel energy.

The technologies are explained later in the Eco-energy zone section. However, it is pure mathematics: the efficiency of solar-energy production is increasing from 15% to 45% and the advanced multijunction technology makes it nearly 98% efficient, which makes it very competitive to nuclear and fossil-fuel energy.

In simple terms, instead of paying off the cost of investing in renewable energy in 18 years, it will be paid off in less than six years. It will also provide us with free electricity for at least 25 years maintenance-free. The cost to the consumer will be as low

LCOE ($/MWh)

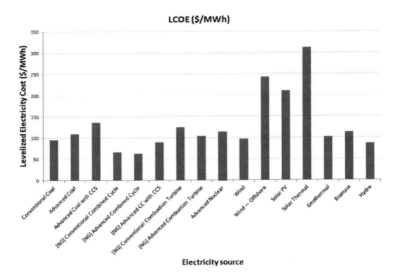

*Figure 4 Cost comparison of electricity sources in KW/h[4]
Renewable energy is getting cheaper than nuclear and fossil-fuel*

as $0.04 (US) for each KW/h, which is much cheaper than what electricity companies charge.

The technical description of the renewable-energy technologies might not be appealing to some readers, but it is necessary to enrich people's knowledge and prove that nuclear and fossil-fuel power stations are not needed and can be replaced by renewable energy sources at a more competitive cost.

The petroleum and electricity companies might not like the idea of replacing nuclear/fossil-fuel energy with renewables and will use their influence on politicians to delay the use of renewable energy to keep the status quo of their business. The ethical suggestion to them is to change their line of business and invest in renewable energy. However, we live in a world of greed and short-term profits, not ethics.

Eco-Electricity from a Water Tower

The tower is a tall, hollow cylinder equipped with water pumps at its bottom that deliver water to the top of the tower's injection system, which sprays the water back down.

The sprayed water evaporates and gets heated by the solar energy of the sun, then falls at a speed of 50 mph to the bottom and spins the turbine generators to produce electricity. This technology works best in a hot, dry climate.

However, in a humid environment, the updraft tower heats the air in glass enclosures at ground level and sends it up to be sprayed down to drive the turbines at the base. This system can be designed to produce electricity 24 hours a day, all year round and is much cheaper than any other source of energy. The Eco-city has a river and so water supply is not a problem and the pumped water is reusable.

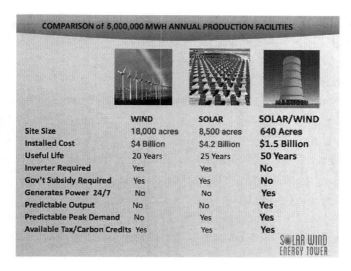

COMPARISON of 5,000,000 MWH ANNUAL PRODUCTION FACILITIES

	WIND	SOLAR	SOLAR/WIND
Site Size	18,000 acres	8,500 acres	**640 Acres**
Installed Cost	$4 Billion	$4.2 Billion	**$1.5 Billion**
Useful Life	20 Years	25 Years	**50 Years**
Inverter Required	Yes	Yes	**No**
Gov't Subsidy Required	Yes	Yes	**No**
Generates Power 24/7	No	No	**Yes**
Predictable Output	No	No	**Yes**
Predictable Peak Demand	No	Yes	**Yes**
Available Tax/Carbon Credits	Yes	Yes	**Yes**

S☀LAR WIND
ENERGY TOWER

Figure 5 Water Tower Comparison[5]
Electricity cost's comparison with wind and solar energy

Eco-Electricity from Solar Energy

The sun's hourly radiation of free energy exceeds the consumption of the 7.5 billion humans in a year. Still, with all that technology at our disposal, less than 1% of the energy used worldwide comes from solar power.

The desert receives solar energy on each square kilometre that is equivalent to 1.5 million barrels of fossil fuel. Moreover, if we multiply the solar energy received by the area of all deserts worldwide, the results would be that the solar power produced in one hour over the deserts would provide hundreds of times more than the whole world uses in a year. In simple terms, the deserts could produce much more solar energy that could be produced by petroleum.

Solar technology varies from the basic, mono-crystalline photovoltaic (PV) cells, which are 15% efficient, to the multijunction concentrators, which are 44% efficient. There is also the theoretical 95%+ efficient pentacene-based PV cells, which are now very expensive, but mass production will make them much cheaper and able to compete with the traditional sources of energy.

Another type of solar power is the heliostat, which is a reflector mirror concentrating the sun to boil oil, generating steam and drive turbines to produce electricity more cost-effectively. Hence, there is no need for the gas-fired power stations that pollute the environment.

Producing electricity during the day needs storage batteries so it may be used at night, instead of feeding the power grid and repurchasing it when needed. Moreover, there is no reason to create added taxes like the 'green tax levy' in the UK to subsidise the electricity companies for loss of income from supplying less power.

Most of the solar panels are stationary. However, by adding stepper motors controlled by a computer program, the solar panels will rotate and track the sun to increase their electricity output by 32%. There are diverse types and they are more-efficient systems that require less land and investment to generate higher output, especially when using a sun-tracking heliostat tower structure that uses mirrors as light collectors reflecting the beam to a solar tower.

There are many applications for the heliostat, depending on its design and this ranges from producing light, electricity, heat and a fiery furnace that reaches 3,500°C to melting glass, iron or other materials. So, there is a way to replace the burning of fossil fuels to generate high temperatures and avoid polluting the environment.

A small heliostat could be designed as a solar-power-tower system, fit on the rooftop of a commercial building instead of occupying hundreds of acres and generate electricity to heat or cool a building. A large heliostat can supply electricity to a community, village, city or power plants.

To utilise the electricity day and night, efficient thermal-energy-storage technology, such as molten-salt storage, molten silicon technology or an equivalent, will be required.

Eco-Electricity from Space Solar Satellite

Clouds can be a problem for solar energy, reducing the sunlight and the night hides the sunlight away, but what if we placed a terrestrial solar-energy satellite equivalent to the size of the International Space Station (ISS) above the clouds or built solar stations on the moon? Then we can produce electricity from renewable sources 24 hours a day, which is freed from changing weather conditions and we can abolish the use of fossil fuels and nuclear power plants for good.

The US Naval Research Laboratory (NRL) has tested two prototypes of what it calls a 'sandwich' module. One side receives solar energy into PV panels and the electronic circuitry in the middle converts the electric current produced from the PV cells to a microwave frequency.

The other side of the sandwich's antenna beams a 2.45 GHz microwave frequency to a particular receiver station only, which asks for it from a specific location on the ground.

So far, the terrestrial solar-energy satellite is the cheapest source of energy and has enormous potential for the future. If the electricity companies invest in this future technology instead of nuclear power plants, then they will make even more money out of it and become Eco-friendly.

One solar satellite station can give electricity to one million houses for 24 hours a day and costs $1 billion; it is much cheaper than any nuclear power plant or fossil fuels and much safer for the environment.

The Shimizu Corporation in Japan announced plans to build a solar strip across 11,000 miles of the moon and to transfer energy through microwaves and laser light to earth. The future is bright for energy from the sun and there is no need for non-renewable, polluting energy sources.

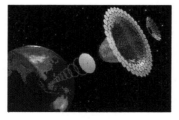

Figure 6 Solar Power Satellite[6]
It can light up 1 million homes at a $1 billion cost

Eco-Electricity from Wind Turbines

Wind turbines were initially called windmills and it is an old concept that started before Christ's era to grind grains and pump water. The first practical wind wheel was invented by the Greek engineer Heron of Alexandria in the first century AD, which used a wind-driven wheel to power a machine. Using wind turbines to generate electricity started in Denmark and Scotland in the 19th century and it was limited to producing a few kilowatts.

More recently, in the 21st century, the giant wind turbines are capable of producing megawatts instead of kilowatts and are used in many countries. The Danish built the Vestas V164 in 2016, which is a giant wind turbine that is 220 metres high and 164 metres in diameter and generates more than 9MW of power, which enough to supply electricity for more than 3,000 houses or many industrial factories.

So, why don't we use the wind energy to supply our farms and industries with electricity? Of course, sometimes the wind stops and we have to use additional alternatives that rely on the sun, geothermal energy, tidal waves or other renewable-energy technologies.

There have been many advances in wind-turbine technology in both conventional and unconventional systems. A company called Sheer Wind in the USA claims to have a new wind-power-generation technology that is up to 600% more efficient than traditional wind turbines.

This wind turbine uses Invelox technology, which is a wind injection system and can generate power from winds as gentle as 1 to 2mph. It does it by capturing passing breezes from any wind direction at the top of its 50-foot tower. The wind is funnelled down towards the bottom, through an increasingly narrow space and when the air is compressed, it speeds up a series of small turbine generators to convert the wind into electrical energy.

In time, chimneys on top of houses and vents on top of buildings could be replaced by some kind of an Invelox technology to generate a much more efficient conversion of wind energy to electricity than the traditional wind turbines.

The Invelox technology can be used in the Eco-city, as well as the giant 9MW wind turbines for the industries and the farmers can erect it in the fields to benefit from free electricity without occupying much of their lands. The giant 9MW wind turbines could also be installed at the Eco-city's perimeters or in the Eco-sustenance areas, in addition to installing other systems like water towers. These systems work on low wind speeds, to supply electricity to the industries, street lights, electric trains, buses and other vehicles.

If wind turbines are not pleasant to the eyes, we can easily erect silent, designer wind turbines on each roof and on the sides of each street.

Figure 7 Archimedes Turbine[7]

Figure 8 Helix Turbine[8]

Designer wind turbines are silent, efficient, cost-effective and beautiful like sculptures

Eco-Electricity from Geothermal Energy

The magma of the earth's core produces more energy than all the nuclear power plants on the entire planet.

The magma continually produces heat from the natural decay of radioactive materials such as uranium and potassium. This heat naturally flows to the surface by conduction at a rate of 44.2 terawatts (TW) / hour and is restocked by radioactive decay at a rate of 30TW/hour, which is more than double the world's entire energy consumption.

As of 2015, the global geothermal-power capacity amounts to 12.8 gigawatts (GW) and only 6.5% of the total global potential has been used so far, but more projects are on their way to reach 17GW by the year 2020.

In the UK and in some areas in the USA, the mean annual ground temperature at 15 metres deep is from 9°C to 13°C and hence is colder than the air in summer and warmer in winter. So, if we can live underground or in a basement without the need to heat or cool our living space, we do not need to spend money on electricity.

The simplest, shallow geothermal energy is gained by digging 5 to 10 metres into the earth, where the temperature is consistently between 10°C and 16°C in some areas and there is no need to generate electricity.

Shallow geothermal energy can be used for warming the house floors and to keep the gardens' raised soil beds at a steady temperature all year around. The French built underground cellars to keep their wine at a constant temperature all year round without having to invest in an expensive air-conditioning system.

However, for the substantial conversion of geothermal energy, digging deeper for a hotter temperature becomes necessary to convert pumped water or steam to electricity by using it to propel turbines that drive motors. The cost of power production depends on the geothermal activity of the geographical locations. In volcanic areas such as Iceland, New Zealand, North Italy and other such countries, it is easier and less expensive to use geothermal energy. In Iceland, most electricity and heating supplies are from a geothermal renewable energy source and not from fossil fuel.

Technically, there are three basic designs for geothermal power plants that pull hot water and steam from the ground. The depth required for generating cost-effective electricity depends on the geology and energy requirements.

The most straightforward design is dry steam that goes directly through the turbine to rotate a motor, then into a condenser to convert it into water. The second method is to de-pressurise the hot water or 'flash' it into steam, which can then drive the turbine. The third approach is called a binary cycle system. The hot water is passed through a heat exchanger, where it heats an isobutene liquid in a closed loop. The isobutene liquid boils at a temperature lower than water and converts into steam to run the turbine.

The geothermal gradient has an average value of 26°C per kilometre, so the deeper we dig, the higher the temperature we get till we reach the core of the earth at seven million °C. However, in practical terms, for some areas, to reach 76°C a depth of 1.8 kilometres would have to be dug to produce 23MW of heat and 24.1MW of electricity.

Commercial companies inject pressurised, toxic fluids to fracture the rocks to extract shale gases and that might cause seismic activity in the form of unpredictable earthquakes. The process releases harmful gases and if they are not captured and re-injected into the earth, they become harmful to the living beings on this planet.

The control standards for deep geothermal energy should put the greenhouse effect before profits and commercialism, where long-term safety comes first at any cost and not the other way around. Rooted geothermal-energy plants and shale-gas extraction are not recommended to be built in the Eco-city's housing areas to avoid the possible geological disturbance of the earth's surface and earthquakes in extreme cases. Therefore, the geothermal power plants should be constructed outside the Eco-city or in the energy sustenance area if proven to be safe.

The advantages of geothermal power are the use of smaller areas of land and 20 litres of freshwater per MW/h versus over 1,000 litres per MW/h for nuclear, coal or oil power stations and has almost no harmful impact on the environment.

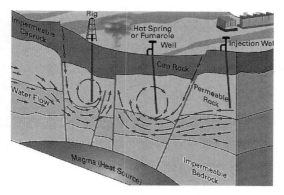

Figure 9 Geothermal Energy[9]
The core of the earth can generate electricity for the whole planet

Tidal Lagoons and Sea-Wave Power

We should take advantage of the sea that surrounds countries such as the USA, the UK, Australia, Japan and many other countries. It is about time we stopped using nuclear power plants and fossil fuels and instead use the sea's tidal waves as the most significant power station on the planet.

The combined energy production in the UK from gas, steam, coal, nuclear, hydro, wind, solar and others is about 396GW per annum. In the USA, it is about 4.5TW and China has the largest production at 5.5TW, while the global potential to generate electricity from tidal waves is much more than humankind needs and consumes.

However, geographical position influences the production capacity. Some locations can generate more electricity than others, depending on the tidal rise and fall and the strength of the waves.

The estimated electricity generated from the coastline of the USA could be 2,100 TW/h from tidal waves and many feasibility studies are showing it is possible to produce hundreds of megawatts in each project or bay. However, they have not tapped into this abundant energy source of the sea and, although a few small projects have fed the national electricity grid, it is still a drop in the ocean.

Several technologies can utilise the tides and waves to generate electricity. There are a few projects around the world producing hundreds of megawatts, but it is a small percentage and must be used to its full potential.

The question is, why do electricity companies do not invest enough in renewable energies? Perhaps, in more enlightened times of humankind and when ethics rise above the greed for money, they will go Eco to produce electricity from renewable sources.

When renewable energy is mass produced in much more efficient ways, it becomes cheaper, greener, a longer-lasting investment and more ethical. All that it takes is for the politicians to encourage companies to go in this direction and for people to use renewables only.

Interestingly, in June 2015, the Department of Energy and Climate Change in the UK granted planning permission to construct the first tidal-lagoon power plant in the world and planning for six more. Each tidal lagoon would have a capacity of 320MW. I hope this technology will become the future for replacing nuclear and fossil-fuel sources of electricity, once the influence of the traditional electricity companies diminishes and politicians become more ethical.

The tidal lagoon is at Swansea Bay in South Wales in the UK. The bay has the advantage of tides rising from 7 to 9 metres high. It is 11 kilometres long and is used for recreation, preserving marine life and farming fish to eat. The electricity is generated from 26 low-head belt turbines under a 550-metre-long concrete-housing structure. Each turbine is 6 metres high and 18 metres long and is capable of generating 16MW/h, which is double the 8MW/h capacity of the largest Danish wind turbine.

As the tide rises, the wicket gates close to create a sea-water level difference and when the gates open the water flows forwards and backwards to rotate the turbine clockwise and anti-clockwise four times a day. The low-head belt turbine drives a motor to generate electricity.

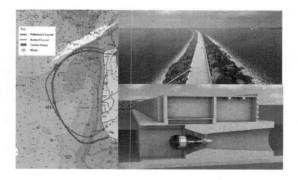

Figure 10 UK Tidal Lagoon[10]
Planned current capacity is 320MW/h

I hope projects like this become international, costs less and are subsidised by governments, unaffected by the influence of the traditional electricity companies.

Nicola Tesla, the inventor of today's alternating-current (AC) form of electricity, wanted to convert lightning into electricity. He died in 1943 without achieving his dream of giving free electricity to everyone on the planet. Electricity companies have made profits of trillions from his invention and he died impoverished in a hotel room.

PART 11

Eco-Water Zone

Whenever there is water, there is life and healthier water is needed for a healthier life.

The Eco-water-plant and its administration might need half a segment of the Eco-sustenance area, but this will also include the Eco-river, agricultural water towers, the Eco-city's pipes and support for the Eco-homes water equipment to constitute the Eco-water zone.

Water purifies our bodies and we should add a re-filtering system before the water reaches the drinking tap to ensure its cleanliness and optimal distillation at the closest point of use.

When people are well off, they can afford to buy healthier bottled water or install a water filter in their house to purify the water supply and rid it of the excessive chlorine, other chemicals or solid residues.

However, if someone cannot afford to buy cleaner water, they might become vulnerable to pollutants or undesirable chemicals injected into the supplied water pipes that worsen the health and participate in the causes of diseases or ailments.

In the Eco-city, the water quality would be under strict control and checked from source to destination. The water systems and pipes are designed to ensure healthier water. The Eco-water-plants will collect the water from the Eco-city's river and treat it for drinking, washing and irrigation. Therefore, three types of water purification systems will distribute the water at various locations, depending on its use.

For Eco-hygiene purposes, natural and safe materials are used for Eco-pipes that do not corrode or cause any harm to the health. The best material to be used in manufacturing the water pipes for drinking water is wood, like in the old days or bamboo tubes, but they might not be practical to install in our modern civilisation. Hence, a high-quality, pharmaceutical-grade polypropylene (PP) is the next preferred choice for drinking water, washing and irrigation pipes. Other types of Eco-friendly materials, such as fibreglass, could be another option.

The drinking-water plant may inject controlled amounts of the nutritional minerals found in natural spring water or the sea to provide high-quality drinking water, which is also to be used for cooking and is better quality than bottled water. However, the water will undergo more soft filtering at each house. Note: The Eco-city's water supply is a backup and an added source to what each house can collect and filter from the rainfall, as I discuss in *Ecolism 4*.

There are many technologies for processing water to suit the requirements, depending on the water source and type. In the Eco-city, water is collected from the rainfall all over its streets, is passed through channels to its river, suitable pumps collect the water from the surface of the river and it is transferred to the water plant to process for various applications.

The water-treatment plant processes the pumped water from the river and injects chemical coagulants and flocculants to settle down the solids present in it. After handling the removal of solids, the water is re-pressurised to remove fine solids through dual-media filters. Then the bacteria are killed by using any of the various methods available. The water passes through filters to remove the fine residuals and eventually gets fortified by a mineral-injection system to make the water healthier for drinking and cooking.

The water for washing is either extracted from the unfiltered water before injecting healthy minerals and after killing the bacteria and removing the residual particles or an entirely separate water plant can be purposefully built to treat it for bathing and washing, with less purification.

The water for irrigation that is sourced from the river and other places can be injected with fertilisers suitable for agriculture and pumped in bigger pipes or channels into the Eco-city's gardens and to the streets for trees and bushes. The water can also be pumped to water towers closer to the agricultural lands for irrigation and the aforementioned updraft water tower also needs water to generate electricity.

PART 12

Eco-Industrial Zone

Henry Maalouf declares:

Employ locals and buy local products to protect your country's ecosystem first, then worry about others.

The Eco-city concept is to live in a more economical way for longer sustainability and this means living within our means without unnecessary extravagance. Hence, we must reduce imports and increase exports, manufacture most of what we use and buy local products even if they are more expensive and less efficient. It is the best way to create more local jobs instead of causing a burden on the welfare system and taxpayers' money.

If we buy a locally manufactured car instead of importing one, we keep the locals who built it employed. However, if we buy an imported one, then we are keeping others employed and making the locals redundant and unemployed. It is the ethical thing to do to buy local and employs locals as part of our loyalty to our Eco-city and fellow citizens. Consequently, this will help the local economy to grow and take care of our wellbeing in return.

In the Eco-city, the Eco-industries are light ones and create environmentally friendly products. They are more economical because they last for a longer time and are higher quality and that is what makes them excellent value for money. Moreover, these are what we should label Eco-products. The Eco-industries will primarily manufacture what the Eco-necessities for the Eco-city are. The Eco-lifestyle does not need luxuries or convenience tools.

Although it is hard to draw a line between what is an Eco-necessity and what is a luxury, it is evident that since we can use a knife to cut a potato it is an essential tool, but the other peeling gadgets become an unnecessary luxury.

The Eco-industries' products we should choose are those that will help us to be more efficient in using our efforts and time. Things like electric bicycles or transport vehicles, which help us to get to work in ten minutes instead of walking for an hour and that is what becomes an Eco-necessity, not a convenience or luxury.

A computer to store, communicate and process myriads of information that our brains cannot easily handle becomes an Eco-necessity, compared to using a pen and paper. The internet is an amazing, super Eco-necessity. It helps us to get an education at home, work from home, communicate with the world and saves us time and money from not having to travel.

Also, using Eco-friendly materials is at the heart of the Eco-manufacturing principles. For example, instead of making a car using metal for the body frame, which is not an Eco-friendly material, we can achieve the same goal by using fibreglass made from hemp as a natural and renewable raw-material source, so we should use more Eco-friendly products.

Apparently, a fibreglass car frame is not as rigid as metal and cannot withstand the higher impacts at faster speeds. In this case, we should not manufacture the car to go faster than the speed at which it can withstand an impact. Consequently, we should adopt all the roads to suit such a design for a car and apply more safety measures to the roads, such as sensors for emergency stops.

The Eco-city is an environmentally friendly city and vehicles powered by fossil fuels are not allowed. Therefore, we must adapt our lifestyle to use electric vehicles to minimise the greenhouse effect that negatively affects climate change on our planet.

The essential Eco-industry factories to build for the Eco-city are timber factories. The Eco-recommendation is to buy timber trees from areas where three trees are planted for each one cut. Then, in the timber factory, the wood is cut and shaped for the prefabricated walls and beams for the Eco-homes, while the leftovers are processed for furniture, cavity insulation, tables, beds and whatever the need arises for.

In Germany, one of the small carpentry factories for prefabricated houses can produce two houses a day, but to build the Eco-city we need larger wood-processing plants that can produce hundreds of prefabricated, flat-pack houses a day. Recyclable papers collected from around the country and other materials from trees can be compressed to use for insulation.

After building the Eco-city, some factories can be converted to different industries or used to build prefabricated houses and other products for other cities. Once we have built the houses, then we must manufacture furniture – such as beds, chairs and sofas – plus the bathroom fittings and kitchen appliances – such as fridges, cookers, washing machines and glass or ceramic utensils.

However, manufacturing devices and appliances requires the use of metal, which is not an Eco-friendly material and we maybe have to use such materials until we find alternatives. The industries and businesses running in the Eco-city should adapt and change their line of business to manufacture what is needed in the Eco-city and comply with its Eco-principles. For example, factories can manufacture fibreglass instead of metal to be used as body frames for electric cars, investment in fossil fuel or shale gas should be replaced with investment in renewable energy and so on.

There are many innovative UK industries, such as Dyson, which can adapt their manufacturing capabilities to build any appliances as required for the Eco-city. It is prudent, when the Eco-city needs more than one million of each machine or appliance for its internal use, to get them at a discounted price. However, when selling outside the Eco-city, they should be sold at a higher price to make more profits and pay more taxes.

Sometimes, we may use utensils to cook for ourselves, instead of eating in the cheap Eco-city restaurants or buying a ready meal from the Eco-food stores. Metal is not Eco-friendly material compared to recyclable glass and most eating or cooking utensils can be made from glass or ceramics or use wooden spoons and plates.

Therefore, we must build glass factories to manufacture the cooking utensils to use for food, water containers and glass windows for the houses. Glass is an Eco-friendly material, which is recyclable and reusable. However, manufacturing glass needs heat to melt it and we should not use fossil fuels for this. Therefore, we can use heliostat sun concentrators to create the required heat from the sun to melt the glass and comply with the Eco-standards.

One of the most important industries is manufacturing electric motors for many applications and the main one being for vehicles, including trains, buses, cars and motorised bicycles. This industry will remain sustainable and will supply the world with electric motors of all sizes and Eco-friendly electric vehicles.

The UK imports cars from Germany, France, Japan and Korea with an estimated value of £70 billion and the USA's car imports are about $170 billion. With this money invested in the local manufacturing of electric cars, more local jobs can be created and a lower impact on climate change can be achieved.

The Eco-city relies on being self-sufficient with renewable energy and it makes sense to set up factories to manufacture solar panels and wind turbines for its one million houses and to sell to other cities in the world. One of the main tasks for the Eco-research-and-innovation-centre is to create advanced technologies for renewable energies and electric motors.

It is wiser to think ahead, be more advanced than other countries and create newer, more-efficient technologies instead of relying on buying old technologies made in Germany, China and elsewhere.

Commercial solar panels and wind turbines are less than 15% efficient, but there are types that are 45% efficient and researchers show us that advances in multijunction solar cells and the material used can make solar panels more than 90% efficient. Similarly, a different type of wind turbine has much higher efficiency than the traditional ones.

In the Eco-city, the minimum standard should be 50% efficient solar panels and when they are mass produced locally, they become commercially viable. Similar endeavour should be applied to wind turbines. Eventually, the solar panels and wind turbines become cheaper, with a better return on long-term investment, to encourage companies to invest in Eco-factories for renewable energy instead of relying upon nuclear plants or fossil-fuel supplies.

The priority in the Eco-city is free electricity to help industries, businesses, front-line services and the residents to use their appliances, machines, equipment and other necessities. Electricity is a necessity for survival in modern civilisation, just as food and water are essential for human survival.

To kick-start the Eco-industries in the Eco-city, let us take the following example.

Each family of four in the Eco-city needs four visual display units (VDUs) or computers. The computer is multifunctional with internet access used for TV channels, internet, telephone or voice over IP (VOIP) and other video-conferencing communication. Therefore, the VDU should be manufactured in the Eco-city as a multifunctional VDU computer to be called an Eco-personal-computer or Eco-PC. The Eco-PC should be connected to the Eco-city's Eco-ICT-data-centre to use a personal virtual computer desktop running on the Eco-city's servers in the Eco-ICT-data-centre. The virtual computer runs any required computer application or program for private, educational and commercial use. Also, it shows TV programmes and movies instead of using traditional TV broadcasting methods.

The point that can be taken from this is that four million people in one million Eco-homes are a bargaining power to buy the cheapest, mass-produced, local products to sell to the Eco-city to kick-start the manufacturing process, then they can be sold elsewhere and be competitive.

Before we begin manufacturing Eco-products, we must create better products than the existing international ones. Hence, the Eco-city has an Eco-research-and-innovation-centre to design the best rather than copying the others.

PART 13
Eco-Innovations

When building a new Eco-city, it would not follow the old traditions of using bricks and mortar, blocks or stones as a commercial housing developer would do. The Eco-city would be built with a new vision, a logical concept and with the latest Eco-technologies that are unique. Before building anything, we should create an Eco-research-and-innovation centre to design the latest and most advanced technologies.

Look at the wonders of the world, including the pyramids; although built thousands of years ago, we are still fascinated by them now. Check out the Greek and Roman empires and what they have built that we still admire.

Jacque Fresco in the USA was an Eco-visionary genius who designed the Venus project for futuristic Eco-cities and he wrote: "The Venus Project proposes an alternative vision of what the future can be if we apply what we already know to achieve a sustainable new world civilisation. It calls for a straightforward redesign of our culture in which the age-old inadequacies of war, poverty, hunger, debt and unnecessary human suffering are viewed not only as avoidable but as totally unacceptable. Anything less will result in a continuation of the same catalogue of problems inherent in today's world."

Jacque Fresco made beautiful designs for Eco-cities, but some economies cannot afford luxuries and beautiful designs.

Therefore, we need a practical, easy and standard design for prefabricated homes that anyone can build by simply following the instructions. The Eco-concept is that each family must have a house not a flat, have an edible garden and become self-sufficient.

The Eco-research-and-innovations-centre should design not only the whole infrastructure of the Eco-city but also every detail of every house and all the things to use, reuse and recycle. At the same time, the innovative ideas and systems could be sold and spread across the world as Eco-products and Eco-designs.

The Eco-innovations will need Eco-investments and Eco-industries to produce such inventions and products. Moreover, what will help is that the Eco-city will be the first consumer for whatever its one million houses need and this will encourage investors to participate, sell to the Eco-city first to cover their investment costs, then sell the new, innovative Eco-products to the rest of the world.

The Eco-innovations must be unique and well-advanced; therefore, the researchers must examine all the available technologies in the world, select the most suitable ones and adapt them and enhance them to suit the Eco-city's requirements and Eco-standards.

The Eco-city will support professors, scientists, innovators and inventors from all over the world, giving them facilities to help them to create better innovations and inventions that will advance humanity in more-civilised, Eco-conscious ways.

Eco-Innovation Ideas

The innovation ideas are the starting point to change the traditional use of human tools for new and better ones and are not limited to the Eco-city's requirements. It will help the Eco-industries to sell new types of products to the world and become more competitive.

Electric Driver-less Cars

Innovative research is required to cover the vehicle's body with solar paint or cells and possibly micro wind turbines could be fitted in front of the engine to generate more electricity when the car travels faster. Moreover, realistically, the most efficient battery and motors would need to be invented and installed in an innovative, active aerodynamic design with a light fibreglass body instead of metal.

The most successful driver-less cars developed by Tesla and Toyota are available at a prohibitive cost. The self-driving features include about 19 proximity sensors, such as cameras, radar and lidar (infrared laser light). The passengers can call a driver-less car, like calling a taxi, by using a mobile app on their phone or start a car, warm it up and bring it from a parking space to a required location.

One of the current autonomous control software applications was developed by Mobile Robotics Group from the University of Oxford as a pilot. However, in time, all developments and enhancements will become more efficient after extensive testing. In the innovation centre of the Eco-city, hopefully, these advances will continue.

The roads and streets in the Eco-city must be designed to respond to the sensors, cameras and radar/lidar of the autonomous cars. The sensors must respond to light reflections, road markings, sudden obstructions, night conditions, fog and extreme weather. It should be easily overridden by the driver or come to an emergency stop if one of the sensors does not detect clear surroundings or detects a malfunction.

Driverless-cars are often used in airports, smart cities, Eco-towns, parks, golf courses, university campuses or similar. However, Tesla is selling cars that match petrol-powered cars in shape and speed and can be charged from various small, roadside charging stations. Alternatively, we can charge the car's battery overnight at home.

There is always a concept for futuristic design; the challenge is to make the future the reality of the present.

Eco-Trains

The Eco-trains are better off underground, beneath the main roads, where they will be unaffected by snow or extreme weather. The trains run on electricity supplied by the energy zone of the Eco-city. The seats must be higher than standard ones for the passengers to be half seated to save space. There would be rows of seats on both sides and two rows in the middle, back to back, joined to each other to save on wasted space.

There should be no space to stand up and a seat for every passenger. Each must have a seat belt for protection from sudden impacts or emergency stops. The Eco-train doors must open opposite to a door on the platform to allow passengers in and leave no chance for accidents or somebody jumping in front of the train, similar to the Jubilee line in London.

Eco-Buses

A bus has a massive volume and all its sides plus the roof should have solar panels or solar paint on them to produce electricity and charge its batteries when the sun is shining.

The roadsides will have electric charging stations at bus stops to enable the electric buses to charge their batteries when needed. The bus's body frame should be a new, innovative design with thick, fibreglass panels that will make it lighter, so it will consume less electricity and become more efficient.

The Eco-city's transport system will be safer than other cities and the buses can be driven in the slow, wide lane at 30 to 40mph for extra safety. The buses could also become driver-less (autonomous) for added security.

Eco-Cycles and Eco-Scooters

There have been many advances in cycles from using the Danish wheel to lighter and more powerful battery-driven ones. The requirement is to adapt those technologies to the Eco-city's infrastructure and add sensors for alerting the driver that an emergency stop is needed upon detecting a possible collision with other objects.

Eco-Glass Containers

Plastic and metal containers are not Eco-friendly and therefore must be replaced with wooden, paper or glass containers. The glass jars must have a mechanism that extracts the air when pushed down to preserve the food in it longer, be easy to open, have an airtight seal and be easy to close.

Eco-Kitchen-Utensils

Cooking pans and pots made from glass, ceramics and clay are Eco-friendly and new Eco-products must be tested to ensure that they last for many years. This material is non-stick, needs only a little oil, needs less heat to cook and cleaning it is a simple wipe. Therefore, it is economical, healthier and Eco-friendlier.

Other tools, such as a combination of a fork and spoon with a cutting edge like a knife, all in one, could be innovated, but should not be made from metal. It should be from ceramic, glass, wood or similar.

Eco-Carrier-Bags

Plastic bags are not Eco-friendly and they are becoming the biggest pollutant of our environment; they must be forbidden instead of selling them. It is appalling that plastic bags end up in the sea suffocating the beautiful dolphins. They must be replaced by bags made from hemp fibres or cloth materials, wooden baskets, glass containers, fortified paper bags tested to carry x amount of weight without breaking or anything that can be recycled after extensive use.

Eco-Electric-Storage-Heaters

Old night storage heaters in the UK use bricks to absorb the heat when the electric filaments heat up and this is old technology. Nowadays, we can use rare minerals or a particular type of salt to store electricity and heat, then release them when needed.

In the Eco-homes, solar panels produce electricity during the day and store it for use at night. Therefore, we should invent a combined electricity-and-heat-storage unit, shaped like a wall-mounted hot-water radiator, to operate as a battery and heater that releases energy on demand.

Eco-Video-Jukebox

The old, coin-operated, phonographic music jukebox could be reinvented to have new functions. The old vinyl records, CDs and DVDs can be replaced with large, terabyte-storage hard disks to hold millions of music videos and other data. It should be able to store all the songs in the history of the world and continuously be updated with the latest music videos, accessing the internet, YouTube and other music video TV channels.

It could also have a unique search engine to check if a song or video is in the local storage and retrieve it more quickly or search the world to find it; the search facility could be by the singer, genre or by writing a few words of a song.

One innovative idea is to convert it into an instant video dating machine. It should have a webcam and a website for people going to a pub or tavern to launch a video session through which they can talk to other people in another pub to see if they like and wish to date each other.

Using coins to operate it or charging for use is old technology and could be replaced by charging a debit or credit card to use the video jukebox to pay for every minute of use.

Eco-Multi-Cooker

The researchers will work on enhancing the pressure cooker, so it can steam vegetables, preserving as much as possible of the nutritional value, making them more economical to use with minimum wattage. It must have additional features such as a scheduler, automatic time setting for each recipe and automatic temperature adjustment depending on the type of food and cooking method. The Eco-multi-cooker should also bake meat, cook pizza, fry with no or minimal oil and boil eggs, along with other necessary features. There are already such multi-cookers on the market that eliminate the need for ovens.

Eco-Motors

An Eco-motor should be universal with variable speeds, step-up controls and multi-voltage input and output. It should have a fail-safe and a cut-off thermostat to prevent overheating or burning the wires, causing it to malfunction. Several standard sizes can be designed from those suitable for electric drills, vacuum cleaners and appliances to those suitable for vehicles small and large.

Eco-PC

Henri Maalouf declares:

> *Why buy many devices if they can be replaced by one at a lesser cost?*

An Eco-PC with a VDU must have all that a personal computer has: a video webcam, microphone, speakers, storage, card reader, access ports for USB and HDMI, Bluetooth, Wi-Fi and others. An Eco-fibre-optic-cable from the Eco-ICT-data-centre will provide the Eco-PC with access to the internet and computer programs. Other models for universal use can be designed to be compatible with all other international systems.

Eco-Printers

Printers nowadays are all in one, with a scanner, copier, fax, printer and card reader and are ridiculously cheap. However, manufacturers make money from selling expensive ink cartridges. The Eco-printer must use newer technology that uses cheaper ink and provides reasonable printing quality that is not necessarily more than is needed for home use. Innovative designs of 3D printers must be encouraged for various robotic functions to support innovators in building samples of their ideas and concept designs for evaluation.

Eco-Cards and Eco-Card-Readers

Standard credit/debit cards have machines to read them. However, in the Eco-city, there are four different types of Eco-card for various purposes and types of accounts. These are the ECDV, ECDL, ECDB and ECDE, as mentioned in *Ecolism 1*, the Eco-social-economic system book. The information on each Eco-card is replicated from the Eco-city's website and will need a larger storage space than a USB storage stick. The current standard for a credit/debit card holds a small amount of data, but the Eco-cards need to store a more substantial amount of data for a lifetime's history for someone's health or accounts.

Therefore, the requirement is to modify or invent a smart card reader that can read the data from the cards and synchronise it with the data stored on the Eco-city's website. The technology already exists but must be adapted to the Eco-socio-economic system of the Eco-city and the software applications that go with it must be created.

The technology of a 20MB-capacity smart card might not be enough for storing a lifetime's information. Therefore, the smart card reader must have a slot to attach to it a micro SD card that can store from 256GB to 2TB of data and if someone needs more than one card, then additional ones would store newer information, like having a new passport, but keeping the older one attached.

Someone in the USA wanted to implant a chip under the skin of each human that would contain a massive amount of information about the individual; this technology is available. However, this is very dangerous and intrusive in the wrong hands and limits people's freedom. In today's technology, a one-cubic-centimetre chip can process information 100 million times faster than the human brain, so imagine what the technology could do.

Eco-Furniture

The Eco-home is a multipurpose home designed for more than merely living and sleeping. It is for work, studying, experimenting and much more, as mentioned in *Ecolism 4*. The Eco-home is an open space, including the bedrooms, except for the bathroom.

Most people, generally, do not use beds during the day. So,

to use the space for another purpose, the beds should be foldable against the wall. Hence, the available space could be utilised for a small children's nursery, workshop, entertainment and other functions. At night, the beds can quickly drop down and have a covering canopy, for a couple to sleep on. It is an economical way to build a house with no internal separating walls between the rooms and so be able to use the limited space for other useful functions at different times. An innovative person could create furniture that could convert to sofas during the day and beds at night, which is easy to do. Even King Henry VIII and other kings had a canopy bed 500 years ago, but we do not need that for luxury; we are trying to economise and distribute the wealth, so more people can live better.

Eco-Appliances

An Eco-city will need many appliances, such as fridge/freezers, cookers, washing machines and others. The innovations centre must reinvent all the Eco-products required locally and internationally.

They must be more economical, durable, efficient, good value for money in the long term, carry an Eco-label and have an international reputation. The Eco-products must be better quality and although they would be more expensive than the Chinese products, they would last longer and be cheaper in the long term.

The West cannot compete with the Chinese in manufacturing cheaper products, which are cheaper in the short term, but become more expensive in the long term. Therefore, the good-value-for-money products last longer and cost less over time and this is how the West can compete with the Chinese.

There are no limits to what people can do and the ideas they can imagine. There are millions of talented people around the world that should be supported to enhance the lives of the human race.

Eco-Software-Applications

The Eco-city will need an army of computer software programmers, for the Eco-city's websites and the Eco-city's applications that will be used by the Eco-council, Eco-businesses and industries, then continuing beyond the Eco-city's fences and out into the world. However, what makes the Eco-city's software programmers more successful than others are the following:

First, they should be more efficient, cheaper and good value for money. They should compete with Indian code writers and the world's best hackers.

Second, they should invent a new and more-efficient programming code or language.

Third, they should modify the characters of the language and keep it a secret to make it more difficult for hackers to crack.

Fourth, they should reverse engineer all the applications used in the Eco-data centre and rewrite them or unify all apps to use the same clean code unknown to global hackers and so on.

The Eco-city will have significant hardware-buying power for its data centres and could request that manufacturers modify the hardware design to accept different coding that cannot be used elsewhere for better security and more control.

PART 14

The Eco-ICT-Zone

Henri Maalouf declares:

Computers are a colossal extension of the human brain.

The Japanese company Fujitsu invented the 'K' computer, which is four times faster and holds ten times more data than the human brain. However, it consumes more electricity than 3,000 homes, while the human brain needs only a little flow of blood, a few chemicals and only about 20 watts of energy from food. The biological process of the human brain produces electrical impulses that move around the 100 billion nerve cells to think, analyse, process information and make intelligent decisions in a fraction of a second.

Google and National Aeronautics and Space Administration (NASA) have announced that the D-Wave X2 quantum computer is 100 million times faster than a conventional computer chip. The quantum computers may, theoretically, solve specific problems in a few days compared to millions of years on a personal computer. Eventually, microcomputer chips will simulate the biological nerve cells' functions, beat the human brain's processing power and replace human intelligence with artificial intelligence (AI). Currently, computers use binary code, but when scientists replace it with deoxyribonucleic acid (DNA) code and different chip or cell material, then the efficiency of computers will multiply a thousand times.

It is terrifying future; imagine in 100 years' time if the animals have become extinct and people have replaced them with robotic ones, what might they do to us if they learn the animal predator-prey instincts?

However, life goes on and let us think about what we can do now to organise ourselves into humane societies doing what helps our progress, with a view on future technological advances.

Creating the largest Eco-ICT-data-centre is vital for the Eco-city, not only to serve the four million inhabitants and the surrounding Eco-industries but also to open its services to the rest of the world. The computers and the internet are our cheap secretaries, consultants and knowledge hub for most of what we need to know, learn and communicate with others.

The IT infrastructure allows us to have virtual meetings with others across the world, without travel or physical contact and it is our mouth, eyes, ears and gateway to the world.

The one million Eco-homes will be suitable for accommodating families of four and everyone should have access to the internet. Hence, four million Eco-PCs will be necessary for the residents only. Moreover, no less than one million will be needed for work in the industries, services, schools and administration. Therefore, an Eco-PC for each user, working as a smart terminal connecting to a virtual desktop computer (VDC) at the Eco-ICT-data-centres is essential for the Eco-city's Eco-socio-economic system.

All the Eco-PCs in the Eco-city, including services, businesses and industries, will connect to the data centres via Eco-high-speed-fibre-optic-cable and have access to all the applications that might be required by each user.

The sizeable servers at the data centres, with the associated infrastructure, will store and stream, via the Eco-high-speed-fibre-optic-cable, all the required software applications to each Eco-PC. In this manner, they will also provide TV channels, internet, phone, VOIP and video conferencing to enable each person to enjoy watching movies, learn from educational programmes and communicate with the rest of the world so they can work from home and make money.

The data centres consist of numerous sections, each one a hosting area for one of the multiple clients, which are isolated from each other, including areas for the residents' network, administration, Eco-businesses and other companies outside the Eco-city. The hosting infrastructure allows each company's networks and systems to be separate from the rest, controlled by their IT professionals and running their approved applications.

Considering the size of the solution to meet the requirements for millions of Eco-PCs inside the Eco-city, the potential for hosting cloud-computing services for companies outside the Eco-city and the central government, the Eco-ICT-data-centres will become the largest in the world.

The IT professionals must be locally trained by the Eco-ICT-university and locally employed, except where specialised skills are needed for specific tasks. No outsourcing is permissible. Every IT professional must be vetted and continuously watched for ethical conduct and each software application will be decoded and scanned for malicious software code to ensure security and prevent cyberattacks exploiting internal loopholes, if there are any.

The Eco-city will buy the best hacker appliances for its data centres' defence to prevent hackers/crackers from accessing the data centres and enhance its security. Also, it will employ the best professionals to set them up in the most secure ways.

The servers (big computers running the software programs)

will be larger than most modern mainframes, such as Hewlett Packard (HP) Super-domes, Google supercomputers or equivalent. All the servers will be connected via fibre-optic cables for maximum speed and the data centre will have large-bandwidth internet cables connected to many internet providers to access the rest of the world.

The Eco-ICT-data-centres will offer companies flexible pay-as-you-use tariffs for accessing their virtual desktop infrastructure (VDI) computer systems and pay competitive fees for their applications to be supported by the Eco-city's IT professionals. The Eco-ICT systems will function similarly to Microsoft Azure and Amazon AWS cloud services to make it more economical for companies to host their IT infrastructure in the Eco-city's data centres.

The Eco-city can offer global and local companies telephone-call services (call centres) for sales and support via its large pools of Eco-sales-force staff and will also be charged per call depending on the level of duty or task.

The pools of workers can consist of anyone who lives in the Eco-city, including the disabled, elderly, part-time workers and lone parents. The Eco-call-centre could become the largest in the world and the most competitive, highest quality and good value for money. This system will attract businesses from all over the world and each Eco-city inhabitant could work in any spare time they have available to optimise the productivity ratio of each person.

The teams protecting the IT systems from cyberattacks use the best and most-advanced appliances, protocols, software, strong encryption, anti-virus software and the most-trusted local professionals to shield the data centre from any security breaches.

The green Eco-city's Eco-ICT-data-centres can be in two

or more scalable underground areas to save on cooling costs. The ground above it should be covered with sun-tracking solar panels and wind turbines, which will charge a massive store of batteries or molten-salt cylinders to provide free electricity. It must also be supported by backup generators and a connection to the power grid could be installed to ensure continuity.

The Eco-ICT specialists and call centres' employees will deliver income for the Eco-city to pay for the investment in the data centres and keep the locals employed after training them in the required skills at the local Eco-ICT-university for the supported software and hardware vendors, engineers and developers.

The IT experts and call-centre staff may compete globally and accept a lower rate because they live an Eco-lifestyle, have much lower outgoings, offer excellent value for money and are available 24/7 as certified security-cleared professionals.

The incoming calls for the call centres will be distributed across the Eco-city and directed to groups of flexible workers using a telephone hunt service (if one person does not pick up a call, the call automatically transfers to another person or a group and whoever answers first gets paid for answering the call). The Eco-homes will have dedicated phone numbers to receive calls and can use cheaper VOIP to cut down on telephone-call costs.

The applications and computer systems will always be load-balanced and distributed between the two data centres, for continuous 24/7 availability and to avoid disruption by any disaster recovery procedures, breakdowns or maintenance requirements.

The Eco-ICT-professionals will always share and document their technical knowledge and give feedback to the Eco-ICT-university so that they can amend their training programmes and software to suit businesses' requirements.

The design of the Eco-ICT-data-centres will be a job for the professionals. However, it will be a modular design with shared services. The standard Microsoft Windows operating system and Microsoft Office applications, along with anti-virus, security and authentication software, will be the standard design and universal for everyone.

It can be one big mainframe, HP Super-dome, Cisco all-in-one enclosure or an equivalent, for a large group of people or a company, as isolated units. Each unit may share resources with others for economic reasons yet maintain independence for security concerns. This modular system is necessary for scalability and stepping up or down as needed.

The specific applications for each business can be isolated physically and virtually for each company or group of users. It is like a building with many floors, which has restricted access to each floor and also has many apartments, where each has a separate door with hierarchical security-access levels. Allowing access to each will require a key that changes often and part of it will be auto-generated every 30 seconds using a fob or equivalent device.

The Eco-ICT-data-centres will create jobs for hundreds of thousands and will also generate billions of pounds sterling to pay back the investment and make significant tax revenue for the government. Currently, the British government spends more than £33 billion annually on IT projects, while local companies outsource their IT overseas, making hundreds of thousands of the locals redundant and still pay billions for unreliable outsourced services. The Eco-city can give better value for money and save billions.

Artificial Intelligence (AI) and DNA Coding

At the beginning of this chapter, I said, "*Computers are a colossal extension of the human brain*" and now, with AI, the challenge is to control a creation that will become smarter than the creator. I also talked about the Fujitsu 'K' computer's processing power compared to the brain and also about NASA and Google developing supercomputers.

Although I touched on the subject earlier, I feel more needs to be said about the future of AI software and DNA coding. For those who understand a little bit of mathematics about Arabic numbers, in that they are based on ten digits (0 to 9) and out of this base we create tens, hundreds, thousands, millions, billions, trillions and so on.

However, in computers, we use base two, which is bits 0 and 1, like a switch: on and off. However, then we create a byte formed of eight bits and this gets increased by repeatedly multiplying by two to form 16, 32, 64, 128, 256 and so on. With this system, we created computers faster than the human brain and with much more speed and memory capacity.

Now, imagine if we use DNA coding based on four bits instead of two, then we start from four and repeatedly multiply by four to make 16, 64, 256, 1,024 and so on. However, manufacturing computer chips (integrated circuits [ICs]) has to change each transistor from one input and one output controlled by one gate to multiple inputs, outputs and gates.

Then the processing power and memory capacity will exceed the human brain in a small mobile phone that we can carry around with us to tell us anything we want to know and help us with making wiser decisions. However, we can hopefully create an ethically controlled AI with red lines that it cannot cross. Otherwise, we lose our freedom to our creation. It is like a father controlled by his children and who has lost the will to think freely.

With such technology and future advances, NASA and others can create spaceships to match the aliens from outer space and explore more galaxies. Robots will roam the earth as acceptable human shadows, programmed for specific tasks; for example, policing, bodyguards or personal assistants.

Most humans believe the 5,000-year-old story in Genesis that God created the earth, sun and moon, including Adam and Eve. Others believe in the evolution of natural selection and that humans evolved from chimpanzees in a six-million-year process of evolution. There are many TV programmes of released unidentified-flying-object (UFO) files and ancient aliens' history, which suggest that aliens visited the earth, built the pyramids, have done many unknown things (including tampering with human DNA) and have created us to mutate to various images.

Whatever the argument is about the creation of humans, they are advancing in technology amazingly fast and one day will they will even be able to create life itself or match their creators. However, the bitter fact is that humans remain insufficiently morally advanced and that limits their progress to faster evolution.

Figure 11 Airbus Flying Car[11]
Drone flying cars and Jet packs are now reality, not a James Bond's movie.

PART 15

The Eco-Agriculture Zone

We can modernise the use of agricultural land to provide food throughout the seasons by using geothermal energy to warm the temperature of aquaponic systems, domes or greenhouses in cold seasons and add fertilisers or manure to keep the soil warm and fertile.

We can dig tunnels 8 metres deep, covered by glass that is a pyramid shape or dome and grow food under a steady temperature all year around for areas covered in snow. Also, we can use natural light bulbs that simulate sunlight in dark places.

The British domes of the Eden Project are a good example of growing any food in any season at a controlled temperature. Moreover, they use geothermal energy to keep the domes warm in colder seasons to save on electricity costs.

Self-sufficiency in agriculture is essential for national security. However, some countries can produce food cheaper than others. The geographical location and the climate of each country is a significant factor in the mass production costs. Therefore, people should adapt their eating habits to the available local produce. However, this does not mean that they cannot exchange food produce with other countries. What it means is trying to be self-sufficient first and using any available agricultural technology to achieve this goal, then making trade deals that do not threaten the income of local farmers.

The farmers can utilise renewable Eco-energy sources to supply power to their farming enclosures, vehicles, water pumps and accommodation. Farmers can surround their farms with Eco-efficient designer wind turbines to generate electricity. The Danish-built 9MW wind turbines may supply adequate electric power to a large farm.

Obviously, relying on the wind as the only source may not always produce electricity or allow enough to be stored in sizeable thermal storage systems or batteries. Therefore, the farmers can use combinations of other sources, such as geothermal plants and sun-tracking solar panels spread on top of the barns or housing accommodation for the workers.

There are many innovative technologies available for farming to increase their outputs during the seasons and help the nation to become self-sufficient. The agricultural technologies – such as geodesic-dome solar greenhouses, horticulture, hydroponics, geoponics, aeroponics, aquaponics and others – enable farmers to grow in all seasons.

It is true that in hot or tropical countries some fruits or vegetation does not need such technologies. Agricultural products can be naturally and cheaply grown, then exported at a lower price than it costs the locals to grow them. The self-sufficiency principle is that national protection comes first at any cost, followed by maintaining the trading balance to ensure that protection.

The farmers will need vast agricultural lands and machinery to cultivate the mass production of commonly consumed crops such as wheat, rapeseed, hemp, soya beans and others. In the Eco-city, the Eco-home's edible gardens will take care of the rest of the fruits and vegetables. The streets will have fruit trees or berry bushes on their sides, the Eco-city's perimeter will have cattle on its river banks and the rivers should be used to farm fish. This will provide most of what the Eco-city needs and ensure self-sufficiency and protect the local farmers.

All the agriculture and farming areas, from hanging baskets to gardens and the vast agricultural lands inside and outside the Eco-city, comprise the agriculture zone. The challenge is to distribute the plants and livestock needed by the Eco-city across the areas inside and outside the Eco-city.

Eco-Agriculture for Better Health

The Eco-concept is to live in a cleaner environment, eat healthier and naturally grown organic food. Therefore, in the Eco-city, harmful chemicals are not allowed because of their adverse effects on human health, even if the effects are mild and people do not feel their immediate effect.

The herbalist's approach to treatment for ailments is using a herbal medicine that slowly cures not only the targeted organ but also all the surrounding ones. On the contrary, synthetic medicine cures a targeted area quickly, but may have about 12 side effects that cause progressive damage to many other organs.

As an example, a cholesterol pill stops the production of the excess cholesterol from the liver but does not stop the production of low-density lipoprotein (LDL) and does not stop eventual clotting of the arteries that may result in a need for a heart operation. No matter what scientists claim, many people have suffered as a result of such treatment. On the other hand, a natural herbal remedy with a specific diet and exercise treats the liver, thins the blood, helps the rest of the digestive system and prevents a possible heart operation.

Naturally produced food is always more nutritious and has fewer side effects. Hence, pesticides and genetically modified organisms (GMOs) can also be harmful in the long term and may cause serious diseases such as cancer. The pesticides may kill some insects and living organisms and also cause cancer, a reduction in fertility, endocrine disruption, autism and other diseases. Although genetic modification (GM) is the lesser of the two evils, it still causes toxicity, health risks, allergies and environmental damage to the ecosystems.

Even if a pesticide causes severe health issues, including cancer and genetic damage, governments still allow it, because of the influence of its manufacturers.

No matter what the argument and conflicting opinions are about pesticides and GM food, the wise choice is 'if in doubt, leave it out'. Pesticides are toxic chemicals that should not be released into the environment they kills not only living organisms on the crops but also the tiny ones living in the human body.

I know from personal experience that when I eat commercial, mass-produced bread, which is injected with 18 chemicals to have a longer shelf life, I suffer from an upset stomach and allergic reaction to it. However, when I eat organic bread from sprouted grains naturally grown and free from additives, then I feel healthier.

There are many pesticide companies in the world and there are especially big ones in Germany that produce hundreds of pesticide chemicals and declare that they are safe. However, the evidence is overwhelming that they are not safe from the increase in cancer ratios; lowering of antibiotic resistance and increases in the number of incidents of autism, Alzheimer's and other diseases. It is business as usual in the unethical and immoral behaviour of corporations that put profits before the health and the welfare of human beings.

There are many safer solutions to protect crops from harmful insects, heat waves, cold weather and other potential future climate-change effects. We can grow them in protected enclosures and install electronic devices that transmit high audio frequencies, which are only heard by animals and repel them from coming to agricultural areas and harming the crops.

The following domes are examples already used on a minute scale and there are other projects growing food underground using bulbs that produce light similar to natural sunlight.

Figure 12 UK's Eden Domes' Agriculture Project[12]
Grow any food any season at a controlled temperature in a dome

Eco-City Domes Idea

Figure 13 Japanese Domes for a village[13]
These domes can be constructed in many shapes and forms

Eco-city domes are just one of the ideas that could be utilised to build homes quickly, economically and more environmentally friendly.

If we cannot plant three trees before we cut one to build Eco-homes from timber, then the alternative is to build Eco-homes and cities similar to Japanese dome houses.

Cutting trees without replacement and destroying forestry reduces the CO_2 consumption and negatively affects climate change. However, the Japanese dome houses use a specially designed expanded polystyrene (ESP) insulation for the walls and this material may not be environmentally friendly. Although this material is 98% air, it is still made from petrol, is non-recyclable and hazardous and ends up in landfill waste. This material can be replaced by polylactide (PLA) made from an organic source, hemp fibre or more environmentally friendly materials.

A dome house can be built in a few days, is assembled on site and it is effortless to learn how to build it. Therefore, building Eco-city could be done in less than a year.

We must explore alternatives to the traditional materials used in buildings to stop creating more damage to the environment. What scientists predicted 30 years ago about climate change has started to be very noticeable in the form of heat waves burning forests, giant tidal waves, a rise in the level of the ocean and melting the glaciers. Governments are influenced by business lobbyists, politics and money to stay in power at any cost and will never care or listen. It is up to people to become genuinely environmentally friendly in everything they buy, build or do, including voting for the right politicians.

However, most people either ignore it or do not care and will remain polluting the environment for years to come. I hope our civilisation evolves quicker in the right direction before humans cause their own extinction.

Endnotes

1   Figure 1 Fast Train to Shanghai: https://commons.wikimedia.org/
    wiki/File:Shanghai_maglev.jpg
2   Figure 2 Slow Train to Katowice: https://commons.wikimedia.
    org/wiki/File:Very_slow_train_to_Katowice.jpg
3   Figure 3 Climate Change: https://climatesolutionsandanalysis.
    wordpress.com/tag/conduction/
4   Figure 4 Cost comparison of electricity sources per KW/h http://
    lagmansnatursida.se/dbarkiv/2017/vecka02/db17jan13.htm
5   Figure 5 Water Tower Comparison http://solarwindenergytower.
    com/images/tower_comparison_2017_v2.jpg?crc=4145998403
6   Figure 6 Solar Power Satellite https://www.nrl.navy.mil/news/
    sites/edit-www.nrl.navy.mil.news/files/archive/pressreleas-
    es/2016/04-16r_Space_Solar_372x252.jpg
7   Figure 7 Archimedes Turbine https://www.thearchimedes.com/
8   Figure 8 Helix turbine https://www.mwps.world/wp-content/
    uploads/2016/06/savenius-wind-turbine-e1458584029914.jpg
9   Figure 9 Geothermal Energy https://myecocity.co.uk/wp-
    content/uploads/geothermal-layers.png
10 Figure 10 UK Tidal Lagoon http://www.bristol.ac.uk/media-
    library/sites/cabot/images/Lagoon%20Image%20Cabot%20
    Website.jpg
11 Figure 11 Airbus Flying Car https://www.airbus.com/innovation/
    urban-air-mobility.html
12 Figure 12 UK's Eden Domes' Project https://www.edenproject.
    com/sites/default/files/biomes_0.jpg
13 Figure 13 Japanese Domes for a village http://www.i-domehouse.
    com/page02.html